SPIRITUAL CURRENCY
LIFE'S CAPITAL

Karren Whiteley-Brooks

T0293874

UBP

Hero/University of Buckingham Press, 51 Gower Street, London, WC1E 6HJ
info@unibuckinghampress.com

Print ISBN 9781800319561
Ebook ISBN 9781800319554
Set in Times

CONTENTS

DEDICATION

I would like to dedicate *SCLC* to the mothers in my life; my mother, Jean Whiteley, who taught me about energy and how to persevere and become more me; my Nan, Lilly Whiteley, who showed me the spirit of play and mother earth, who showed me the value of exuberance.

FOREWORD

As a man who considers himself to be a people person and appropriately self-confident, I attribute my enjoyment of connection with people to work developed with the author over the last fifteen years.

There is no doubt in my mind, that Karren has helped me to expand my people and communication skills, and generally my level of self-belief.

The skills of which I write include spiritual understanding, the development of powers of concentration and physical and mental agility.

As a whole, I now recognise in myself that, thanks to the author, I am someone who has gone through a long evolutionary process of self-development, i.e. generally enjoyed an upgrade!

I am fortunate to have had in my life, access to the knowledge and the teaching of the author, which the reader of *Spiritual Currency – Life's Capital* will happily discover.

J. Adrian Watney
The Mercer Company

SPIRITUAL CURRENCY

Every currency has a symbol which helps one recognise the implied value. As a country's Gross Domestic Product (GDP) expands and contracts, so does the value of its currency. The icon or symbol of a currency is emblematic of that particular money, and the first currency itself was invented some 3000 to 4,000 years ago to help with exchange.

Exchange is basic to both commerce, as well as Spirituality and Consciousness. The analogy of currency to our basic life's capital is a representation of the wealth of our spirit and the height of our consciousness. Money is the focus of numismatics, a term derived from the ancient Greek *Nomisma*.

We have chosen the mathematical symbol of a Mobius Loop (∞), similar in appearance to the Greek character Omega, which both embrace the concept of continuity and a system which flows without end and appropriately represents Spiritual Currency.

> *"....but money has become by convention a sort of representative of demand; and this is why it has the name 'money' (nomisma)-because it exists not by nature but by law (nomos) and it is in our power to change it and make it useless."*
>
> *Aristotle, Nicomachean Ethics*

9

INTRODUCTION

I would like to thank you in advance for trusting me by reading this book. I would also like to congratulate you, if, like so many of my readers, you have begun this book in the quest to improve your life, personal growth and contribute to the well-being of our world. You are the type of person I enjoy meeting and with whom I enjoy sharing life's experience. It is my intention to have a conversation with you; this conversation has been inspired and enriched by many friends and teachers who have encouraged me to consolidate my thoughts in book form. I am most grateful for their friendship, insights and contributions.

Like one's savings account, which increases and decreases with economic currency, similarly, our Spiritual Currency fluctuates from positive and negative encounters during life's journey. It is my intention to grow my Spiritual Currency and yours through future iterations of this book. You may enter into this exchange by accessing the link below and contributing your thoughts and experiences:

www.spiritualcurrency.co.uk

It will be those reader's submissions which I will incorporate in future editions, because we can learn from each other and our spiritual growth is life's challenge and journey. You may not have time or believe other people would be interested in your perspective (and I can certainly relate to that)… it has taken me many years to find the time and confidence to formulate my thoughts in written form. You will not find either a theist or atheist viewpoint in this book, but you will be challenged to refine your own explanation of the scientifically proven connectivity which exists throughout the universe. I will, nonetheless, attempt to "converse" with you about SPIRITUAL CURRENCY, which is LIFE'S CAPITAL.

This first edition received no funding from any of the products or systems mentioned. If in future editions those endorsements or valuable ideas are requested by their sponsors, we will gratefully accept donations to the Whitespace Foundation (formed to improve continuing education throughout the developing world).

In the spirit of transparency, and because I always like to understand what to expect when I commit to a book, if you continue to read this book you will be asked to think and explore your belief systems regarding a variety of topics, including Trust, Gratitude, Acknowledgement, Relationships, Sex, Energy, Presence... You will find contemplations which may assist you in evaluating your personal development and increasing and maintaining your spiritual performance.

I thank you again for your commitment to this book and look forward to our conversation. My intention is for you to be even more Y.O.U. (Your Own Universe).

Karren Whiteley-Brooks
Hertfordshire, England – Winter 2020

ABOUT THE AUTHOR

Karren Whiteley-Brooks founded Whitespace at the request of her successful client base from the London Leadership Centre. She is passionate about global consciousness and the neurosciences, which help explain the emotional and mental performances required for the attainment of success and happiness. Karren brings that valuable experience to her advisory services for business executives, legacy families and elite sports organisations and athletes. Karren also founded Innovators Highway, which provides guidance, valuation, and fundraising for entrepreneurs and their Intellectual Property. Each of these offerings is notable for the remarkable breakthrough results achieved with her clients.

I
CREATION MYTH –
SPIRITUAL INTRODUCTION

> *"Please allow me to introduce myself, I'm a man of wealth and taste…"*
> *Mick Jagger, 'Sympathy for the Devil' (1968)*

In the song quoted above and performed for over 50 years by the Rolling Stones, Mick Jagger's lyrics go on to ask, *"Can you guess my name?"* While the song title contains a clue, the answer is more profound and contemplates the devil in all of us. This iconic rock tune takes us on an historical tour of evil events, as evidenced in the stanza: *"Who killed the Kennedys? …after all, it was you and me."*

We all have our own "Creation Myth", and by that I mean how we portray ourselves to ourselves… Jagger sings, *"I'm a man of wealth and taste."* Who do we think and say we are? What are the major influences in our creation? This "Creation Myth" is not the proverbial rib from Adam's side, but our own genesis as we understand it; some of it true; some of it a myth, which we have compiled over our lifetimes. Our personal introductory story, like the Hebrew Book of Genesis, encompasses our sacred narrative.

When we introduce ourselves to others, our "Creation" story may be adapted, depending on the occasion. As we explain who we are, redacted from the composite and complete story, our introduction will contain select and sometimes embellished portions of our personal creation myth. If we are to believe a variety of sociological studies, most new acquaintances make several false statements within ten minutes of their first encounter. Before you answer, "I never lie about my age or my relationship status or my education, etc.," possibly your untruth is more in terms of flattery to the new acquaintance in an attempt to build rapport?

Most of us shy away from "honesty is the best policy" when the norms of social etiquette advise us to avoid revealing anything too controversial. The issue is not only that we lie, but more frequently that we dumb down our creation narrative, choosing elements that will least offend and descriptions of ourselves which produce reactions with less probability to defend. Social introductions become a dance, where we want to engage, but avoid stepping on toes at all costs. Years of repeated conventional wisdom mantras, such as "first impressions are most important", have hypnotised us into recounting personal narratives which are valued for pleasantness and style over complexity and honesty.

We may adopt our personal introduction revealing only partial aspects about ourselves with an abbreviated version. This shorter version is often used in brief encounters such as social and even business situations. This synopsis is sometimes called (in marketing speak) the "Elevator Pitch". Wikipedia defines "Elevator Pitch" as a "short summary... possible to deliver... in the time span of an elevator ride". If, when you are removed from the time-constrained elevator scenario, you continue to repeat to yourself and to new acquaintances only your abbreviated pitch, you may be performing an auto-suggestion which becomes your new reality. In this age of attention deficit, social distancing and political correctness, we may be rapidly homogenising away the more wholesome and important aspects of our being with the intention to "fit in".

Before Continuing: Please access CONTEMPLATION 1. found in the Book of Y.O.U. These contemplations will help track your personal growth and like a spiritual bank statement, begin to reflect the deposits you are making through your quest.

If you have now completed the contemplation by recording your personal introduction, you will have probably included several important aspects about yourself. Have you mentioned any collective or group connections? As an example, did you mention your position in your family or of a religious affiliation or a company or business? If you would introduce yourself by describing your role in one of these collective cultures, you would NOT be unique. Humans are social animals and enjoy being in collective groupings for many important and understandable reasons resident in our DNA. It is when these labels become stereotypes that our quest for spirituality may be hindered.

Our sophisticated Western society has taught us to avoid "pigeonholing" or that narrow definition of anyone which allows us to make a generalised judgement. We nonetheless are drawn to label ourselves and others in some of our/their noteworthy characteristics: such as age (young or old); race (black or white); citizenship (British, American, etc.); sexual orientation (straight, gay, etc.); religious affiliation (Christian, Jew, etc.); job title (Chairman, Director, etc.); and even physical characteristics, such as heavy or fit. The list of labels and collective categories is endless, but the unfortunate result of stereotyping is to agree "not to know what we don't know".

Another example of non-descriptive introductions can be illustrated when we watch the ubiquitous TV talk shows. I saw a good example recently, when the famous singer- songwriter, Akon, was introduced on an American talk show as a proud, young, black Senegalese-American recording artist, who is extremely fit and listed as one of the most powerful celebrities in Africa (Forbes Celebrity 100). This is a lot of information and a variety of "pigeonholes" which don't really allow us to know Akon, or to understand if he is happy, present, connected, intuitive, patient, kind, generous, serene, honest, etc. You choose the virtues or attributes which really define a man and which your philosophy or religion deem to be most important.

Having met Akon, I am happy to report he is much more than just a talented, successful artist, but a very spiritually oriented individual. While we will speak about virtue and religion in later chapters, the QUEST on our journey to build spiritual currency is to know that we don't know ourselves or Akon or any individual whom we define simply in terms of their roles and generic descriptions.

Philosophers have debated knowledge and wisdom and the concept that many people go through life in a condition explained as: "You do not know what you don't know". The connections required to become more spiritual require a diligence to recognize when we think of ourselves or others using superficial, generalised and limiting nomenclature. We must recognise the limitations of knowing ourselves and others when described in pigeonholed convenient descriptions.

When asked "do you know... Mr X?", we may respond in the affirmative, stating "Oh yes, I know him", when in fact our definition of "knowing" is commonly misused and understood as having met someone, although not necessarily having any profound understanding or experience of Mr X and his real being.

Truly knowing is not the normal connection we have with even those we call FRIENDS, because we may be more comfortable only receiving and revealing partial elements between ourselves. We will discuss friendship in more depth, later in the book. Our nurtured friends are the key investments of our Life's Capital.

Possibly you included in your short personal introduction a mention of your family role such as parent or sibling, your business position of manager, entrepreneur or founder? While completely normal, if we define ourselves to ourselves, in terms of our roles, we limit our being. We can only be what we tell ourselves we are. If when you introduce yourself, you say "I am a parent", then those of us who have never had our own children become automatically suspect. If you mention your role as parent in a group of parents and non-parents you may be unconsciously attempting to form a collective ego, especially if you interject statements like "you couldn't imagine" or "you would have to experience it to understand it". You might well think one couldn't understand the importance of being a parent if one never had children of their own; but that is your ego feeding its superiority requirements. You have unwittingly created a "me and them" identity. Parents might even carry over an ego-fuelled superiority role or identity in their relationship with their children.

My business partner has twin teenage sons and enjoys his role as father. He also has been a manager, directing and commanding many subordinates. Having watched him issue commands to his sons, we discussed his role and communication with his children. We came up with the military title of Sergeant Major as an identity. Although he was never in the military, when assuming the role of father he was speaking as someone who issues orders and expects no questions or discussions in return. When he realised that his managerial or Sergeant Major identity was manifesting itself in his relationship with his sons, he was able to separate himself from that role and adapt his behaviour, controlling his ego.

The behaviour of assuming roles is not necessarily negative, but if it is done for ego satisfaction or false or embellished identities, then our being is subjugated and our opinion of ourselves is damaged. Can you identify any roles which you wrote in the first contemplation? Do they define your being? Do you mention those roles because your ego dictates their inclusion? In this age of specialisation, we all need roles or functions in order to compete and be economically productive. But we must separate ourselves from those roles if we are to grow our spiritual being.

It may take the help of a guru or spiritual processor to point out those identities with which we are comfortable. Our self-image may be masking our true BEING. Many times these masks are one's attempt to conceal what we perceive to be our inadequacies. Those masks, which we develop to hide or withdraw from letting others know us, are usually counter-productive to becoming more spiritually connected.

If we begin to think about ourselves, we typically come to a point of personal disappointment. This is completely normal and, when recognised, part of our spiritual growth and evolution. Our inner voice eventually complains with the admonition, which begins with thoughts such as "I should have", and for each of us (depending on our evolving standards) continues with a variety of unfulfilled dreams and destinations which our life's journey has convinced us are important achievements, yet to be reached.

CONTEMPLATION 2: LISTEN TO YOUR INNER VOICE. Please turn to your Book of Y.O.U. before continuing. Thank you.

The challenge of becoming more of oneself is illustrated in the popular saying "comfortable in his own skin", which has come to mean someone who is confident and knows the essence of his being. What skin are we in and are we comfortable? The multi-billion-dollar cosmetics industry perpetuates and stimulates our feelings of inadequacy and sells potions to help us look better. Think of the last person whom you met (face to face) and whom you would describe as comfortable in his/her own skin. Did it have anything to do with physical beauty? Did they project a positive mindset and enviable tranquillity? Did they wear a lot of make-up? We all know that the media and advertisement manipulate images and stylize beauty to sell products. Watch the time-lapse "Evolution of Beauty" (YouTube video produced by Dove beauty products) to better understand this manipulation. Images and fashion are the embodiment of illusion.

We all are a composite of our memories, some conscious and some unconscious, many repressed, in order to avoid the unpleasant event. Those memories can be evidenced in our chosen identities and protective masks which can be conflictive in our communication and connection with the rest of humanity. The following anecdote was brought to my attention as illustrative of my ability to connect: something that we sometimes take for granted, or sometimes fail to notice.

Last year I was sitting in one of London's most beautiful parks, Hyde Park, with some friends. It was a pleasant summer Saturday and one of the unusually hot days for England, and the park was full of people. One child, who was playing on his own under the watchful eye of his father, was at that perfect age of post-toddler, where he could run freely and enjoy the warm grass on his bare chubby feet. I was admiring his smile and innocence from about fifty feet away when the boy turned and waved to me as if we were old friends. His gaze was so engaging and warm that one of my friends looked behind me to see if someone related to the lad was standing there. So evident was my connection, I returned the wave and smile and the lad continued his frolic undisturbed. My friends asked me if I knew him, so unusual was the brief but warm salutation. I replied, "No," but I connected with his being and admired his freedom and happiness. It was my being's attention which connected with the little boy's being. He connected with me because I was open to him in a non-judgemental way. I wasn't worried about some unforeseen danger or trying to engage in some game of my choice, but only connecting. Sometimes wordless introductions may be the purest and most profound.

The exact polar opposite from spiritual connection is evidenced in the information exchange produced from the modern concept of speed-dating. This practice, popularised in the fast-food capital of the world, the US, has spread like a burger chain and is most likely coming to your neighbourhood soon. Speed-dating is where a group of men and women, who don't want to make the investment of time or effort required to understand the essence of their prospective partners, are given around five minutes to ask some questions and introduce themselves before moving on to the next suspect.

The sponsors usually coach the participants to speak about common interests, hobbies and activities and NOT get too personal or intimate. Heaven forbid that they really reveal themselves. This is the tacit agreement which is evidenced in most interactions of repressed beings; that is, we agree "not to know what we don't know". When we look at the conversations, they become ludicrous and superficial, just the opposite of what is stated as the intention of the participants, which is to identify and get to know a compatible partner. The pace of modern society heightens the illusion of communication and connection. Messaging services with abbreviated texting and limited space have replaced love letters, where one can share one's feelings and aspirations. The speed-dating phenomenon replaces repeated conversations and romantic dinners which allow for understanding and emotional connection. This superficial interchange is encouraged by social media, where the digital tagline of "Get Connected" has everything to do with linking over the Internet but little to do with spiritual connection or true understanding.

"He lived a life of passion?" is a question alluded to in the book *Cut These Words into My Stone: Ancient Greek Epitaphs*. Are we living a life of passion? Do we value passion or what are the most valuable attributes as taught by our family, education, society and possibly religion? These epitaphs are illustrative of what was important to the ancient Greeks and contrast with how modern society has evolved to value other attributes. You may, as my editor warned, be repelled by the notion of an epitaph, yours or anyone's, but no one said spiritual growth was easy.

The ideas of knowing, understanding and wisdom, both for us as individuals and for what many humans have described as an omniscient God, are difficult concepts. When we study the great thinkers, the evolution of "knowing" is hard work and many of us would rather exist than contemplate. This is the existence where one is content "not to know what we don't know".

We will speak of death and grief later, but if it is not too unpleasant, ask yourself what virtues would you like to be known for when you are no longer in this body.

The history and evolution of philosophical thought is dealt with in depth by more qualified authors, and spiritual currency is always gained by studying these great debates. My purpose, here, is not to convince you of one virtue above others or one philosophy or religion as preferable, but to pique your curiosity and encourage you to re-investigate your personal preferences and values.

Virtue ethics promoted by ancient Greeks like Plato and Aristotle placed an emphasis on being virtuous as an end in itself and a desirable state of being. Socrates was the first to popularise the notion of "knowing that he didn't know" and died imprisoned with his personal moral code intact. Later philosophers challenged this notion and felt morality should be viewed and judged with an outcome or result in mind. This continues to be a popular notion in our action-oriented Western culture and has been termed "consequentialism", where costs and benefits are more important than any intrinsic or natural law. This notion was made famous by Mr Spock on years of Star Trek television shows when he would say dispassionately, "The needs of the many outweigh the needs of the few."

If a young man came up to you on a street corner and said, "Hello, I am loyal, trustworthy, friendly and considerate," you might well think, "this must be a Boy Scout and I don't need help crossing the road." Early in the twentieth century, General Robert Baden-Powell selected important attributes from diverse and noble cultures, which included the Japanese Samurai, Native Americans, the medieval knights' codes of chivalry and the qualifications for warrior status by the African Zulu tribe, whom he had encountered while serving in the British military. These attributes comprise the Boy Scout Law, which has been translated and adapted in over 150 countries. These laws include "honour is to be trusted, loyal, useful and helpful to others, a friend and brother to every other scout, courteous, friend to animals, obedient to authority, smiles and whistles, thrifty and clean in thought, word and deed". Not a bad list and certainly admirable rules which would help in any young person's quest toward positive growth. However, virtues and adherence to laws or guidelines have evolved in the twenty-first century to be synonymous with being boring or too nice. This repudiation of virtue can be seen in the popular saying, found in a recent article in the English *Guardian* newspaper, where Kevin Mitchell wrote about the British boxer Anthony Joshua, "He is no boy scout and knows how to enjoy himself but…" – the implication being Boy Scouts don't know or can't enjoy themselves because they are adhering to a virtuous code.

On a frieze etched into a portal at the Basilica of the well-known US University of Notre Dame, one can find the motto:

"God Country Notre Dame".

This motto was developed in the Second World War as a suggestion to the students of what should be important during their academic life. Recently an autobiography written by the former president of the University, Theodore Hesburgh, used the same motto in its title. The author, a well-respected educator and statesman, said the words in the motto were his "guiding principles". This is an example of what has been termed by philosophers as deontology or fundamental rights and duties, as our ethical foundation.

Any principles or precepts that guide an organisation throughout its life in all circumstances, irrespective of changes in its goals, strategies, type of work or the top management, need constant review and renewal. Our spiritual currency grows as we challenge ourselves to improve and adhere to our evolving principles.

You may well agree with the fourth-century theologian, St Ambrose, who is credited for saying in Latin, "*Si fueris Romae, Romano vivito more.*" While the context of this quote is found in a treatise calling for separation of Church and State, the common usage has come to mean more than just to live as the Romans, but to adapt to your surroundings and to BLEND. You may put on a mask with your projected identity for your personal comfort and even safety, and so not all masks are undesirable. The Native American Iroquois False Face Society have used masks in their healing process and believe they can hide the sick from evil spirits. While some masks may be healing, many more are limiting us from becoming more present and understanding of our true nature. Ironically, one of the biggest debates in the midst of the Covid-19 pandemic is whether masks are necessary or effective in preventing virus transmission.

The digital age has created new masks by allowing connection and yet eliminating the human element of interaction. On social media like Facebook, status choice includes "It's complicated" as one of the more popular selections. One can infer that the complication is too embarrassing, or our "friend" isn't worthy of a non-masked explanation. The complexity and choice of our smartphones gives us a constantly increasing ability to recreate, inform and communicate at the touch of a button. Our inability to give our attention to a concentrated and more spiritual thought because of the myriad of applications and distractions is the new digital-age mask, which prevents worthwhile and more spiritual interaction.

The American author Isaac Asimov predicted our evolution and dehumanising addiction to technology. Asimov's *Robot* series inspired a variety of films which have explored the evil possibilities which may occur when future machines have no intrinsic ethics or moral principles. Films like *WALL·E*, *Terminator*, *I, Robot* and many others have entertained, while provoking the real question of future potential disasters related to digital advances.

In the TED series on technology of April 2012, MIT psychologist Sherry Turkle, formerly a proponent of digital connections, cautions against the creeping dehumanisation caused by our digital devices. Turkle watched robots replace human interaction and fears for our future. Is technology evil or is humanity lazy? This is one of the questions we need to examine to replenish our spiritual currency.

We began this chapter with a quote sung by Jagger, performing as Lucifer. We have considered our introduction and contemplated our self-image and impediments to gaining increased spiritual currency. I would like to close this first chapter with what I think embodies our ongoing spiritual struggle, as taught by a wise old tribal leader and narrated by George Bernard Shaw:

"A native American elder once described his own inner struggles in this manner: Inside of me there are two dogs. One of the dogs is mean and evil. The other dog is good. The mean dog fights the good dog all the time. When asked which dog wins? He reflected for a moment and replied, the one I feed the most."

2
Y. O. U. –
YOUR OWN UNIVERSE

"Today you are You,
that is truer than true.
There is no one alive who is
Youer than you."

Dr Seuss, Happy Birthday to You!

Yes, Happy Birthday to Y.O.U., which, I like to say, means Your Own Universe. If you can contemplate your original birthday, please try to imagine you begin your Life's Capital account as a Spiritual Billionaire. This is the reverse of how most of us experience our normal economic currency account, where we start with little and grow our wealth during our lifetime by depositing a portion of our earnings from our productivity. If we have been very successful in economic terms, we might even make the lists of the super-wealthy billionaires, and be included with those elite names – Jeff Bezos, Warren Buffet, Sheikh Waleed bin Talal, Sir James Dyson, etc. – most of whom have invested well to attain their moneyed status. In order to explain Spiritual Currency, let us imagine that we begin our current life with a billion *Mobius Life Coins* in our Life's Capital account. Teilhard de Chardin says, "We are not human beings having a spiritual experience. We are spiritual beings having a human experience." As spiritual beings we inherit that connection with our universal consciousness. We are born spiritually wealthy, and our connectivity and awareness of our universe is undiminished from adverse experiences, doubts and regrets. At birth, to paraphrase Dr Seuss, "it's truer than true... no one... is youer than Y.O.U.".

We all admire healthy babies for their innocence, their beautiful skin, their ability to be concerned with only the most basic of needs. I mention "healthy" babies because I realise many developing countries, including Afghanistan, Niger, Mali, Somalia and others, sadly lose more than ten percent of their infants to disease. Many of the babies born in emerging economies are not so fortunate as to be born in good physical condition. Infants who have received the blessings of healthy prenatal and postnatal environments may be thought of as beginning life as spiritual billionaires. Rich in *Mobius Life Coins*, we begin our human life without the experiences which sap our energy and disconnect us from the spiritual universe. These connections are explained by philosophers, scientists, theologians and atheists in a variety of ways, but, it appears, most of these concepts are defining the same spiritual connection. For me, to become more spiritual is to become more connected. More connected not only to our fellow living humans, but aware of everything in our physical and metaphysical universe. So, as babies, we are spiritual billionaires, who begin losing spirituality and connectivity from the moment we are born. This spiritual struggle was explained by the philosopher Kierkegaard as "life can only be understood backwards; but it must be lived forwards".

Many child psychologists who study infants have concluded that babies "assimilate" or absorb input from the moment of birth and, at some levels, even at a pre-natal stage. This absorption and assimilation of sensory inputs can teach babies, very early on, to scream and cry when they want attention. Piaget (the Swiss psychologist, not the watchmaker) stated that children rapidly find a balance between 'assimilation and accommodation'. Many argue that the only original, non-influenced sound humans make is our birth cry and, from that moment onward, infants are reacting to sensory inputs and experiences in order to optimise their survival. Babies are immediately connected to the humans around them. For most infants the main nurture and nutrition source (typically from one's mother) is the strongest connection, but by no means the only source of development. What has been proven, far beyond the obvious survival instincts and family influences, is that babies are receptive and connected to all of humanity. Babies can feel stress and happiness on a spiritual level which can drastically influence their development. The ACE (Adverse Childhood Experiences) chart, which categorises horrendously abusive family situations, also shows that all childhood stress from community tragedies, such as war and forced migrations, can contribute to "health problems in later adulthood". The community and societal connections received in childhood can influence, and indeed trap and sap our life-force particles which we call *Mobius Life Coins*, debiting our Life's Capital account.

The concept of virtual *Mobius Life Coins* thrives in what I have called during my career the "WhiteSpace". It is consistent with, but not entirely explained by, quantum physics, and is described by many scientists as the unseen forces and laws yet to be discovered. It is not to be confused with the God particle, as termed by physicist Leon Lederman, which is more often called the Higgs or Higgs-Bosun particle. This latest sub-atomic particle discovery is not the equivalent of life force particles, represented by *Mobius Coins* but, as science advances, is unusual new evidence of the increasingly unexplainable, which creates more passionate debates as to how everything is interrelated. The vision of our spirituality infused with life force capital does not necessarily prove there is a God in the traditional theological sense but, similar to molecules viewed with an electron microscope, makes one react, as Alice in Wonderland might say, our existence is "curiouser and curiouser".

Just as physics attempts to explain power and energy in the material universe by watching for evidence derived from particle collisions, our life's energy can be explained by the fragments of our spiritual being; called life force particles. The power we have to be aware, communicate and connect is the measurement of our wealth of spiritual currency, and to be esteemed, just as adult monetary billionaires are noteworthy, for their economic and political influence. We all have read or watched or possibly met those individuals who are "spiritual" icons or whom I would deem to be spiritually super-wealthy, as evidenced by their kindness and goodness. When we connect to these enlightened individuals, their spiritual magnetism pays us dividends in *Mobius Life Coins*, pulling us in a wealthier and a more conscious state of spiritual well-being.

The world was considered flat by most of its population only 700 years ago. The conventional wisdom dictated that if you sailed far enough you would fall off the edge. Despite some medieval scientists and sailors who had mathematical proof and visual evidence of the earth's curvature, they seldom raised their heads above the parapet of common understanding. Aristotle, despite his academic credentials, was dismissed for his anti-biblical view of a spherical earth. Today the leaders of modern science, which is constantly evolving and discovering new subatomic particles and positing new laws of physics, are now looking back at renowned scientists of the twentieth century and ridiculing them for their simplistic and deocentric ideas, calling them "flat-earthers". Independent of your religious beliefs and conclusions regarding the creation of the universe, what is inescapable is that the more we know, the more proof exists of both a scientific and spiritual level of human connectivity. Physical human differences of sex, race, fingerprints, height, etc., which can appear remarkable to our senses, are scientifically less distinct; arguing for a collective connection on the micro-biological level, with 99% of all human's genes being identical.

Palaeontologists who are perfecting the Darwinian theories of natural selection currently believe that modern humans,

Homo sapiens, are descended from apes. Creationists, who subscribe to a more literal biblical explanation, argue for Divine Intervention in the origin of man. At the risk of sounding like spiritual politicians, we contend that both creationists and evolutionists can enjoy huge accounts of spiritual currency. If we revere connectivity and kindness, our *Mobius Life Coins* will continue to compound. However, both God-fearing fundamental religionists and atheistic paleoanthropologists can be spiritually bankrupt if they live in a close-minded and disconnected state of "not knowing that they don't know".

For much of the nineteenth and twentieth centuries the debate and differences between scientists and theologians created an expansive gulf. If you believed in a God or supreme forces, you were automatically anti-scientific and less sophisticated. The more quantum physics and genetic research advanced, the more belief in a Supreme Being seemed to wane. In fact, the twentieth century will be famous for the secular development of society and anti-religious movements. Unfortunately, when great scientists and published authors equate belief in any spiritual being as primitive and a "flat-earth" mentality, their scepticism towards any alternative lifestyle and belief system strikes fear in those of us attempting to increase our Spiritual Currency. This inordinate fear of spiritual belief is exhibited by many educated individuals and is as dysfunctional as economic doom-and-gloom merchants, who caution us against investments and advise us to keep our money under the mattress.

In the best-selling book, *The God Delusion*, Richard Dawkins summarises his interesting argument in six easy steps which he believes proves the "God Hypothesis is untenable". These steps take the reader from belief in God because of the amazing design of the universe to complete acceptance of Darwinian theory as destructive to any "illusion" of creation by Supreme invention or intervention. The arrogance of dismissing God because of perceived "truths" discovered by scientists strikes me as ironic, since wise scientists know that theories and explanations are constantly revised and rewritten. What is more disturbing to me is Dawkins's suggestion, as supported by several studies, that "the higher one's intelligence or education level, the less one is likely to be religious or hold 'beliefs' of any kind". The conclusion is that belief in our spiritual universe is tantamount to ignorance, and those of us seeking spirituality are stupid "creationists" and "flat-earthers". Let's keep sailing and searching.

In the mid-nineteenth Century, Charles Darwin argued in his seminal work on evolution, *On the Origin of Species*, that "natural selection" and the "struggle for existence determined the development of all species". Despite zealous atheists using Darwin and evolutionary theories as one of the most important "proofs" that God and spirituality do not exist, they ignore the author and his foundations for the theory.

Darwin was a son of a wealthy medical doctor who wanted his son to become an Anglican parson and sent him to Christ's College, Cambridge. Darwin argued in his examination paper for a "divine design in nature" and saw no inconsistency with a God as evidenced in the natural laws. Although Charles Darwin never became a cleric, he wrote, in a personal letter to John Fordyce in 1879, "It seems to me absurd to doubt that a man may be an ardent Theist and an evolutionist... but... I may state that my judgement often fluctuates... I have never been an atheist in the sense of denying the existence of a God." The explosion of zealous atheists in the twenty-first century may take Darwin as the poster boy for the "untenable" conclusion that NO God exists, but they do so without understanding the "fluctuation" of the great mind of the creator of evolutionary theory.

In Darwin's autobiography his fluctuating judgement concluded that all religions had some validity, although they developed as a "tribal survival strategy" and it is his humility, "to know that he doesn't know", which made his discoveries so important and credible.

Independent of your personal beliefs in God or religion, what appears to be more accepted by both the scientific and theological community is the notion of collective consciousness. In quantum mechanics it is proven that observation can change the particles and physical properties of that which is observed. This is not the philosophical riddle of "If a tree falls in a forest and no one is around to hear it, does it make a sound?" (George Berkeley, *A Treatise Concerning the Principles of Human Knowledge*.) The argument of philosophers discussing our perception versus reality is constantly evolving. What is known is our perception can be augmented by connecting with the universal consciousness. Those of us who take time to invest in our own spirituality receive dividends in better physical health as well as increase in our *Mobius Life Coins*. Independent of whether your reality includes a belief in God or a rejection of a Supreme entity, it is important to know that those are merely personal decisions and typically oscillate over one's lifetime. What is more important is to passionately pursue a reality which includes a dedication to spirituality. "Reality is merely an illusion," Einstein once declared, "albeit a very persistent one."

On any given day some financial guru will extol the best methods to invest for our future economic return. The usual advice goes something like: you must buy a property or invest in a mutual fund or buy gold, etc., despite the horror stories of loss of capital associated with each of these investment vehicles. While many times the risks in these monetary investments are noted, the overriding logic is that to do nothing with your money is to guarantee a loss, due to inflation and accompanying erosion of buying power from our economic currency. Similarly, religions many times argue that their belief systems are the only ways to receive a future gain of salvation, heaven or nirvana.

The exclusionary aspect of most institutionalized religions demands adherence to their dogma as the best or sometimes only way to progress to a celestial return. Not unlike most enlightened financial advisers who counsel asset diversification for investment portfolios, we can look at the best aspects of religions and philosophies while forming our spiritual belief system. The Spiritual Currency account, like our investment account, can take advantage of the diversification of the important lessons from each method or belief system. In later chapters we will discuss some of these techniques and methods for building our Life's Capital account. One of the best ways to release and increase our Life Force particles is by surrounding ourselves with the ideas of the great thinkers and the most spiritually enlightened humans of today.

We are compiling our own list of 'Spiritual Billionaires' and you may wish to nominate candidates for this list of the truly super wealthy:

www.spiritualcurrency.co.uk

If you wish to submit your experience of observing Spiritual Billionaires, we will publish our readers' nominations on our website. It is our intention to honour these people who deserve to be revered and their ideas should be enjoyed in equal measure to those of monetarily wealthy icons. Very few of the economically rich could make our spiritual list, despite their philanthropy.

It is a shame that so much media coverage is spent on the activities and attainments of the economically super-wealthy, when even they understand that their preoccupation with money may make their happiness and accumulation of spiritual currency more improbable. The difficulty for the rich to become spiritual is contemplated in the often-quoted New Testament Synoptic Gospels.

"I tell you the truth; it is hard for a rich man to enter the kingdom of heaven.
Again I tell you, it is easier for a camel to go through the eye of a needle than for
a rich man to enter the kingdom of God."
Matthew 19:23–26

We all have days and sometimes, longer periods where we lack energy. While diet, exercise and sleep, among other health issues, are typically blamed for this human state of low energy, our connection to the spiritual and emotional discouragement of life's travails, may be the more important cause for our lethargy. In later chapters, we will examine human health issues and best practices, offering some of the latest techniques and technologies, but first, let us contemplate a history of one hypothetical spiritual being. This individual's life force particles are the "spiritual tail wagging the human dog"; where their behaviour traps the spiritual currency with little renewal or positive movement in their Life's Capital account.

SPIRITUAL CURRENCY	AGE	LIFE EVENTS
∞1,000,000,000	0	Healthy pre-natal and birth care.
(∞22,000,000)	0 to 2	Infant illness-allergies, no breastfeeding.
(∞12,500,000)	2 to 6	Family moves homes. School changes are unsettling!
(∞8,000,000)	6 to 10	School bullies and teachers' criticism sap confidence.
(∞87,500,000)	11	Repeat 6th grade. Classmates are unsympathetic.
(∞42,000,000)	12	Smoke cigarettes, later try pot.
(∞78,000,000)	13	Quit sport and exercise, gain 20% body weight. Poor, fast-food diet.
(∞90,000,000)	14	Join undesirables, shoplift, harder drugs, E, coke.
(∞120,000,000)	16	Loveless first sexual experience.
(∞80,000,000)	19	Catch unfaithful lover. Lose trust in romance.
∞660,000,000		End adolescence. Enter young adult-hood with little hope or ambition, having lost 340,000,000 *Mobius Life Force Coins*.

SPIRITUAL CURRENCY	AGE	EARLY ADULT LIFE EVENTS
∞660,000,000		Begin adulthood, low self-esteem, little orientation to spirituality.
(∞34,000,000)	21	Made redundant from enjoyable job.
(∞26,000,000)	23	Cheat on romantic partner.
(∞82,000,000)	25	Marry into a co-dependent relationship. Drugs.
(∞58,000,000)	30	Major illness.
(∞73,000,000)	32	Move home and lose friends.
(∞97,000,000)	34	Divorce.
(∞84,000,000)	35	Death of friend.
(∞44,000,000)	36	Continued overweight.
(∞36,000,000)	37	Yo-yo diets and join cult searching for meaning.
(∞62,000,000)	38	Take boring job.
(∞44,000,000)	39	Borrow money, payments stressful.
(∞19,999,900)	40	PROZAC prescribed.
(∞100)	41	He loses his last 100 Mobius Life Force Coins. UTTER DESPAIR

Before our hypothetical individual declares Spiritual Bankruptcy, you may be thinking: what a woeful log of a life's downward spiral. You may have been blessed with better habits and more fulfilling relationships during your life, but recognising past events which may have trapped our *Mobius Life Coins* is one way to recover our spiritual currency and grow our life's capital. We all have heard that death, loss of job and moving home are usually considered the three most traumatic events in a human life. Not unlike the way we study techniques to invest and grow our monetary savings, examining our past and the decisions and consequences of our personal experience improves our access to our life's capital account.

You may not feel like a Spiritual Billionaire just yet, but the previous ledger is another renewal of our intention to improve our spiritual ledger. Just as savings and investments can pay dividends and grow through the compounding of good decisions and budgeting, our personal account of life's capital can increase by self-examination and dedication to spiritual growth.

The studies of neuroscience and neurobiology are constantly mapping and investigating the material brain and improving the understanding of the social sciences of psychology and sociology. These distinct zones of existence are more than just moods, and their existence can be demonstrated on modern machines like Magnetic Resonance Image equipment. The former Soviet Union, in an attempt to maximize sports performance, commissioned a variety of studies which led to the publication of *Individual Zones of Optimal Functioning* (IZOF) by psychologist Yuri Hanin. The IZOF conclusions led to the incorporation of meditation for those sports where accuracy and focus were paramount in performance. Whitespace exists and meditation can assist in achieving these states of optimal performance, not only in sport but in life.

The mind is distinct from the brain, and while stopping brain function would lead to termination of life, the "stillness" or quiet mind achieved in meditation has been shown not only to reduce stress but to improve overall health and performance. While meditation in sport and the pursuit of performance called being "in the Zone" is well documented. The majority of performance attributed to the mental side of sport is understandably a huge portion of our overall success and enjoyment of life.

CONTEMPLATION 3. MINDFULNESS please access your Book of Y.O.U.

The skills required for success in life can be categorised in distinct areas or frequencies which we can depict as colours of the familiar traffic signal: green, yellow and red. When we are in the green frequency, our ability to go forward is unimpeded and our mastery and power are predictive of success. Our green frequency status allows us an abundance of energy, fuelled by our confidence and love for life. Our dreams become goals and we take effective actions and communicate our passion for reaching our targets. We have no qualms in asking for appropriate help and acknowledge those who assist us with sincere gratitude and empathy for their contributions. We are living a virtuous life and deliver what is promised to our companions, becoming trustworthy and valued for our reliability.

Of course, we will have difficulties and challenges, as we attempt to maintain and grow our life's capital which flourishes in the green frequency. Our mastery of areas of knowledge may be limited by our incompetence due to inadequate education or organisation. The dualities of life are normal and our ability to be productive will be hampered by incompletions and our development will be restricted by anxiety.

It is important to understand and overcome the threats to our stability in the green frequency and realise that decisions, acquaintances and environment can drag us down into danger. We can colour this zone yellow, for caution. As we feel our success breakouts, we must recognize the reluctance to "have it". Our power is being weakened by our inability to enjoy and sustain our success. The dynamic contraction of personal power is almost tidal, as our feelings of self-worth can ebb as we doubt our deservedness for success. One of the most important conditions for maintaining Mobius Life Coins is our ability to enjoy our success. If we paraphrase a famous sportswear manufacturer, we can't "just do it", and many times we find it equally difficult to just "have it". A common area for therapists to process is the origination of their patient's feelings of lack of self-worth, which fuels their attraction to failure and sabotages their ability to trust others who may be able to help.

For every level of existence which is positive and contributes to our spiritual growth there is an opposite or at least negative aspect which can undermine our progress and pull us into the undesirable red frequency, where we are prone to mistakes and feel very unlucky. The ability to understand our environment begins with what has been called "presence", which is not just "showing up" or being there, but being aware that we are there. This constant battle of positive and negative elements in our existence means that we function up and down the ladder of skills moving from high functionality (Green) to states of fear and caution which impede our actions (Yellow) and can lead to isolation and hostility (Red), causing immobility and complete absence, the opposite of the presence required to be aware.

This dualism of existential states is a philosophical concept made popular by the medieval philosopher Descartes, who looked at consciousness and self-awareness and made a distinction between our material brain and our mental, thinking mind. Descartes argued that the brain/mind difference proves the existence for what most religions call the soul. Science and neurobiology, more particularly, have argued against this distinction and said that a functioning brain which is material is all that is required for thought and life.

Independent of the philosophical and theological debate, what is irrefutable is the duality of positive and negative forces we are exposed to in our lives which can move us between the green space of a successful and a highly functional state or drag us down into the red space of failure and chaos.

For more information about Whitespace technology and personalized analysis of your own life skills and abilities please go to:

www.whitespaceleaders.com/geniuswithin.html

When we think of spirituality it is oftentimes confused with being removed from the reality of daily life. Many times our mantra may be: "I could be more spiritual if I had more time or more money or fewer worries or less stress." These ideas lead us to believe that a spiritually enlightened existence is the purview of hermits and monks, who have no job or family or daily concerns and can focus on the spiritual and meditate and pray.

Unfortunately, most religions have some founders or current leaders who have created a mystical and more spiritual aura around them, exemplified by their separation from society, only returning to teach or perform miracles which engender awe and worship.

Even non-religious teachers and gurus who are offering tranquillity and motivation typically advertise their seminars in remote locations, mountain tops or water resorts and even call their seminars "retreats". Our modern society has taken separation to ritualistic proportions. Southern Europe, for example, literally closes for the month of August, unless one's business provides services to the tourist and vacation trade.

The Western idea of recreation is to take a vacation. Usually separation from home and daily environment with travel to a different climate, and sometimes culture, is accepted as the ideal "retreat" for our recreation; literally meaning to "re-create" ourselves. Many vacations advertise our ability to rest and reconnect with our inner selves, separating us from the daily drudgery of our homes and places of work. It can be shown that for creativity what is needed is more connectivity (not separation and isolation); yet we treasure our holidays.

While vacations and separation from routine may be desirable for recreating our energy and focus, there is evidence that productivity in fact falls after vacations. In a study published in *Cognition*, in 2010, it stated "Task-Unrelated Thoughts" (TUTs) or daydreaming could lead to better executive performance, and that "vigilance decrement… could be decreased… and that heightened levels of vigilance can be maintained… with the use of brief… actively controlled disengagements from the vigilance task". The further conclusions of the study remind me of my grandmother, who would say, "If you want to get something done, give it to a busy person." While the University of Illinois's study speaks of power breaks, it does not explore the short meditative breaks which can increase our focus and goal orientation.

Henry Ford knew that more hours on the job would not increase productivity and embraced the change from 6 to 5 workday weeks. *Bloomberg Businessweek*, accepting that almost 60% of summer vacationers take some work with them on holiday, published tips for "Maximizing Productivity on Vacation". These tips included taking an eight-foot extension cord and USB stick in order to print important things. The most important tip, which underlines the difficulty in returning to the workplace, advises us to expect at least one hour of catch-up for every day missed before one can fully be "up to speed".

Most of the productivity studies call for focus and goal recognition, which can be related to our quest for Spiritual Currency. It does not require a trip to an ashram in India, although that can be pleasant; what is necessary is the power of our intention to be better and kinder. Henry James said it better than most: "Three things in human life are important: the first is to be kind; the second is to be kind; and the third is to be kind."

We began this chapter with discussion of Y.O.U. (Your Own Universe), and have considered the vagaries of science and religion. If you accept the traditional definition that our universe is the totality of existence, including planets, stars, galaxies and all matter and energy, then science and religion may expand our understanding of that existence. The contemplation of existence is never easy, and philosophers and scientists have suggested that a "multiverse" (many worlds) definition of all existence is most probable. This multiverse theory is sometimes explained as "bubble universes", where other separate space-time entities coexist. These other entities are beyond our comprehension and influence, and may exist as if our universe were one soap bubble and others we couldn't see are floating in another dimension. While exciting and stimulating to contemplate the latest theories, what is clear is that we still don't know all that much, and explanations will continue to evolve and challenge our understanding of who we are and how we are interrelated. The most important concept in growing our *Life's Capital* may be to maintain an open-minded focus on challenging ourselves to constantly evolve our own view of the universe.

Alvin Toffler is frequently cited as stating: "The illiterate of the 21st century will not be those who cannot read and write, but those who cannot **learn**, **unlearn**, and **relearn**. The words in fact came from Herbert Gerjuoy, whom Toffler cites in full as follows: "The new education must teach the individual how to classify and reclassify information, how to evaluate its veracity, how to change categories when necessary, how to move from the concrete to the abstract and back, how to look at problems from a new direction – how to teach himself."

In conclusion, we may consider a medieval theologian and Neo-Platonist philosopher, Johannes Scotus Eriugena. His thoughts on the universe may have even more credibility, because he was first, and always, an Irish poet. "*Natura*", he writes, is the name of the most comprehensive of all unities, that which contains within itself the most primary division of all things, that which is (being) and that which is not (non-being). While "*Natura*" is interesting to contemplate, the inescapable conclusion is that we must make our own way and build our own Spiritual Currency as we replenish and reinvest in our Life's Capital account.

3
RELATIONSHIPS AND COMMUNICATION

"The meeting of two personalities is like the contact of two chemical substances: if there is any reaction, both are transformed."

C.G. Jung

As we look at our own universe and contemplate our relationship with those around us, what is clear is that communication is one of the most important life skills we possess in our quest to increase our connectivity and spirituality. We will discuss the five flows of communication, because these flows are important in understanding our interaction with our universe and increasing spiritual currency. They are as follows.

1. OUR SELF TO OUR SELF – this is the inner voice, the conversation which is sometimes bifurcated into the good angel and bad angel; the internal debate.

2. OUR SELF TO AN OTHER – this is when we speak or indicate through signs and gestures and, indeed, even think about others.

3. AN OTHER TO OUR SELF – when others address us or gesture and indeed, think about us.

4. OTHERS TO OTHERS – while you may not realise the

importance of this flow, what others communicate to others may have a profound effect on our existence.

5. AN OTHER TO THEMSELF – while less directly affecting our existence, what those around us say to themselves and how they think is a major influence in our ability to communicate with them and be understood.

We all think we understand communication, but seldom stop to diagram or watch the different flows and how they affect us and our universe. Jung, quoted above, despite being focused on psychology and famous for his dream interpretations, understood the complexity, on even a biological level, of this human connectivity. Carl Jung is renowned for his exploration of the unconscious mind and the explanation of personality archetypes such as introverted and extroverted.

We all have archetypes which may be both genetically and environmentally developed. An example noted by Jung was, if your family and friends describe you as shy, that repetitive notion can become a reality. We may be asked to portray archetypes, which are uncomfortable or unnatural, and we may have developed identities without stopping to examine our effect on others.

The first step is to begin to answer the question posed by great thinkers since the beginning of time. That is, "Who am I?" Possibly more importantly, who am I telling myself I am? This is the examination of the first communication flow.

Listening to that inner voice and the conversation we have with ourselves is the first dynamic in the most important relationship, Our Self to Our Self. In a variety of therapies and meditative techniques employed by eastern spirituality, the idea of separation from ourselves in order to be able to observe our totality is paramount to understanding and answering: "Who am I?"

In Buddhism, this separation and perspective is often called mindfulness, and is a state of calm alertness achieved by concentration. This state is sometimes called awareness. The concept of mindfulness has been listed as one of the most important states of spiritual growth, and the seventh factor on the path to achieve enlightenment.

Please turn to CONTEMPLATION 2. Book of Y.O.U. to invigorate your senses.

Do you have enough detachment and silence in your daily life to listen to yourself? This is a question which needs to be asked frequently to ensure that we are giving ourselves perspective and an audience to eliminate the frustration of not being heard. It is all too easy to be caught up in our work and life activity and not listen to our inner voice. We all have had the familiar, frustrating experience of trying to speak to someone who cannot be aware and cannot listen. Equally disturbing is not listening to our inner voice by allowing distractions and routine to drown out our internal conversation. Our inner thoughts can be enhanced by meditation, but new evidence shows how that meditation can also increase our connectivity with those around us, giving us more presence and Spiritual Currency.

Deepak Chopra, along with Dr Alva Noë, who wrote *Out of Our Heads*, have collaborated and articulated in defining the collective consciousness and community mindfulness as demonstrated by group meditation. The increase in serotonin levels in the brains of those who meditate at Chopra's centre is well documented. What surprised these neurologists is the measurable increase in serotonin in people who did no meditation but who only encountered the individuals from the meditating group. They believe that this argues for the biological and cellular link of all living organisms, even without physical contact. Each of us can and will influence and affect those around us.

One way to explain this connection of organisms is to view our human moods as if they were a virus. No doubt the community mood can have a viral ability to bring smiles or frowns to those who both directly and indirectly experience positive or negative events. Documented studies have been reported in medical journals from both the US and Great Britain demonstrating an increase in sickness and absenteeism in metropolitan communities on the days directly following a significant defeat of the local sports team. This has been found to affect those in the community, even if they have no interest in the sport or the team. Our spiritual currency can be negatively impacted by an environment in which the predominant mood is depressed and dejected. While we are often admonished to be careful with whom we associate, ancient wisdom translated in many languages teaches that if you "lie down with dogs, you may get up with fleas". The latest neurobiological studies demonstrate the similarity to a viral effect on our consciousness produced by our general environment. Even internet marketing has now included in our vocabulary the term "going viral", which means a rapid and contagious spread of information and connectivity through cyberspace. To build our spiritual currency we must guard against these sometimes-unseen negative connections and build a personal filter to sieve the inputs we are being exposed to on a daily basis. Those around us can transfer unseen "bugs" as if they were a virus, and our awareness of the communication flows will help in our immunisation.

The connectivity of humans with each other is often unseen but evidenced in a variety of interesting ways. It is well documented that women who live in proximity, such as in a dormitory, tend to synchronise their menstrual cycles.

A women's college dorm with over 100 residents participated in a study which demonstrated that, within the first semester of their living together, over 80 % of the female students had periods during the same week each month. Several other experiments demonstrated that the unseen molecules of

the females' excreted pheromones were the chemical reason for this biological synchronisation.

In the US state of California, a study was conducted at the Sonoma State Hospital Brain Behaviour Research Center. Not unlike the way that strong leaders can infect a group with positive or negative viral-like moods, certain females in the studied group appeared to be the catalysts for the menstrual coordination. The pheromones extracted from under the arms of certain women were shown to be more powerful in instigating the synchronicity of periodic coordination with other members in the group.

The proof of molecular interchange between humans is being revealed constantly in the twenty-first century, and science reveals this evolutionary conditioning as a significant part of the instinctual urge to procreate. While Freud became famous for basing many of the human psychological influences on sex, the chemical aspect, which has now been demonstrated, was only suspected when he wrote his theories early in the twentieth century.

Deepak Chopra has an excellent book called *Synchronicity*, which relates a variety of ways that humans are interconnected with each other and their universe. While Dr Chopra relates many neurological connections, the more fascinating aspects of his book demonstrate the unseen or sixth-sense connections of knowing and awareness. These are not magic tricks of psychokinesis-like experiments but the very real way our feelings and emotions connect us spiritually. The stimulation of our brain and reaction to each other can be explained by the chemical changes which are pure science, but the way we intuit and feel those connections may never be fully-understood. While the conclusion of many scientists and theologians is that we ordinary lay people should just take the universal consciousness "on faith", because rational and scientific explanations may never eliminate the mystery of our connectivity. This is the theological argument travelling full circle.

One other important consideration of the first flow of communication we have with ourselves is the detachment required to ignore or silence our inner voice. This is not the healthy perspective of listening and conversing with ourselves by using meditation but by employing external distractions with the consequence of muting our consciousness. The use of opiates and other drugs to dull our senses and allow us to abandon the inner conversation, when increased to an addictive level, can overtake our inner voice and become a physical imperative. But the use of video games, social media and even television can be used to excess rather than spending time listening to our inner voice. By not giving a receipt point to our minds' conversations and concerns, we increase the charge of emotional distress which can lead to dire mental and physical consequences

Who we are in a digital age, where the new reality of technological devices can enhance our connectivity and aid in our communication, was described by Kevin Kelly in *The Technium* as a "self-correcting organism". Kelly isn't referring to software aids like spell-checker or predictive text, but speaks about the "blurring" of the distinction between flesh and blood or physicality with our mind and thoughts and consciousness. We are at an evolutionary and spiritual tipping point in human understanding, where the cynical doubts regarding concepts like soul, consciousness and connectivity are not only being refuted but being proven to exist by technologically advanced devices which can measure and enhance the understanding of the unseen.

We will have more discussion of who we are, but one question which I hope you will continue to ask and will continue to examine is, "Am I becoming spiritually wealthy and increasing my Life's Capital through the compassion and kindness required to improve the community mood?" Like any examination, the contemplation and audit of our Life's Capital will help us understand where we are and where we want to go.

In the examination of the second communication flow, that of Our Self to An Other, being understood, heard, comprehended, appreciated, received, etc., is the one flow that has occupied communication teachers since the beginning of human existence with caveman's first uttered intentions. Archaeologists and sociologists agree that Palaeolithic humans had a hyoid bone, which meant they had a voice box similar to modern humans.

While a variety of theories have explored the development of language and communication, what is clear is that we can make others understand not only our wants and desires but express our emotions and abstract concepts. Humans have been able to do so for at least hundreds of thousands of years. So why can't we make ourselves understood?

UNDERSTOOD – defined as "Past participle, past tense of understand (Verb), perceive the significance, explanation, or cause of (something)".

Words and meanings are the basis of our understanding and need to be comprehended. The "triggers" of certain words may inhibit our understanding and ability to be understood. When the meanings of words and their receipt by those to whom we are directing our communication can be interpreted in a variety of ways, clarity of definition is important. A humorous example can be illustrated by North American tourists who have become identifiable in Europe by their use of "fanny packs", or those satchels worn around the waist and typically supported by one's lower back or what they would term "fanny". Unfortunately, for those so adorned, when travelling to Great Britain, if they were to refer to their bag as a "fanny pack", the reaction would be normally a mixture of perplexity and possibly derision. Considering that the usage of the word "fanny" in the UK is a nickname for the female genitalia and the thought of "packing" it would be even more abhorrent, the trigger or reaction to that word can lead to a variety of unwanted misunderstandings. It is not just the definition or usage of words that can impede our being able to be understood, but the intention and "tone" behind the words.

Certain musically gifted performers and piano tuners have what is referred to as "perfect pitch", or the ability to hear and recognise musical frequencies, perfectly. This awareness and focus allow them to hear when musical notes are out of tune. The understanding and awareness produced by recognising the various communication flows produces in the spiritually wealthy an ability to hear when the tone of communication is "off key" or false.

More subtly, but just as important, are the "triggers" which certain ways of speaking may produce when "An Other" listens to our commentary. Sometimes accents, colloquial sayings and even gestures can not only be misinterpreted but produce in our communication partner an unwanted response which damages our connection.

Many psychologists have studied body language and the facial and physical manifestations of intention and their unconscious expression of underlying emotions with silent communication. Recognising what is the "real intention" behind the words is the core premise in the popular television series called *Lie to Me*, which glamourised this ability to detect untruths by recognising the character's unconscious body language.

The good news is that with heightened spirituality our communication improves, as does the ability to connect on a non-verbal level through intuition and empathy. The expression "see right through me" is one way of describing that feeling when we communicate to another who has amazing intuition and really knows what we mean and what we are thinking. We feel received and appreciated, and that empathy is an inspiring outcome which leads to further communication and takes away any desire to mask our true intentions.

If we have a basic intention to communicate with another human, language may not be necessary where smiles, sign language and thoughts can produce understanding between two people communicating an idea. While the variety of human languages and their development is a mature area of social science, the understanding of telepathy and non-verbal communication is in its infancy.

Another interesting aspect of the five communication flows is that they each have a profound importance in our connectivity with our universe. In our travels the concept of "remote viewing", or being able to see an image or energy without being physically linked or proximate with the object, is one way of thinking about the communication flows. While most of us are sceptical of our ability to "remote view" and much of the world is ignorant of one's ability to influence the outcome of the future, a simple example may demonstrate the phenomenon. We can step back and examine the flows from an objective separation on any subject. Let's pick a common and mundane topic: my impending travel plans, which we can call "*this*".

1. What am I saying to myself about *this*?
2. What am I saying or projecting to "An Other" about *this*?
3. What will they think or react and reply to me regarding *this*?
4. What will, or are, Others saying or thinking about *this*?
5. What will the Other say to himself about *this*?

In order to make *this* more tangible, let us review the consequences of my incorporation and realisation of the five flows, which was instrumental in planning and communicating my intention to visit the Dalai Lama a few years ago. The consequences of my examination may be illustrative of the remote viewing and predictability one can accomplish by contemplating and incorporating the five flows. All of us do this situational examination to a greater or lesser extent. Those of us who work on our communication and awareness may be able not only to see, but to shape the future we are contemplating. Here is one example of how understanding of communication dynamics shaped my future.

In response to one of those coffee-fuelled conversations where a friend asked, "If I could meet anyone, whom would I like to meet?", my rapid response was the Dalai Lama. Initially, it was just a passing comment, but in my mind I was already sure I would meet him, but I hadn't focused on when or where. When we are in touch with our intentions, they are not just fluttering ghosts of thoughts but a reality to be expected.

Later that day, I was sitting on my sofa and my friend texted me and jokingly asked, "When r we c-ing the Dalai Lama?" in a perfunctory message, transmitted well under the 160-character limitation of SMS technology. We had bantered about seeing him and how we would act, but the difference in our situations was my sheer intention. When reading the message, despite the implied humour and scepticism expressed by my friend, my intention and awareness was without any doubt. My thought was emphatic: 'I WILL MEET THE DALAI LAMA."

Soon after the realisation of my intention, events collided to produce an opportunity for me to travel to Germany in a few weeks' time. When to my pleasant surprise I found that the Dalai Lama would be in the same city and at the same conference, I was not shocked but recognised my intentions working. I had not planned to go to Germany and not attempted to synchronise my trip with the arrival of the Dalai Lama, but, as has happened many times in my life, my intentions conspired to make a reality of my thoughts. Coincidence? I think not.

Within a week, members from the organisational management team of the German conference bumped into me in London and described their event in Munich which they thought I should attend. I chuckled to myself knowing that I had invoked these coincidences through my intention. At that time in my life, I was studying Quantum Physics and working on myself to improve and clarify my awareness. We all have these moments of clarity, when our intention becomes reality and which we dismiss and misunderstand as just coincidence. The beauty of recognising the power of our intention is that recognition increases our ability to predict and influence our future.

Despite my recognition of the alignment of my intention with the opportunity to meet the Dalai Lama, the mundane practicalities of travel and budget intervened to dampen my enthusiasm. Having recently invested in a new business venture, I was low on funds and thus needed to find the finance to make this trip a reality. I never doubted I would find the money but needed to plan and communicate my intention to others to produce the desired result. How I thought about the impending trip and influenced others through my communication, both directly and indirectly, by sharing my intentions, assisted in my arriving in Munich.

The conference management team I had accidentally met in London invited me to a dinner on the first night of my arrival in Germany. I had only enough available funds on my credit card to pay for one night at one of the best and most expensive hotels in Munich. The practicality of me paying, I somehow knew, would "just work out". While I was telepathically transmitting my funding requirements to my new friends, another, more mundane obstacle to my continued stay in Munich occurred when I checked in to the popular conference hotel Bayerischer Hof. The manager, who took my last-minute arrival with charm and welcome, let me know that the hotel was over-booked and I would have to find other accommodation for the rest of the week. I knew I would meet the Dalai Lama later that week and my visualisation gave me a sense of calm and the ability to transmit my intention to stay in the hotel for the entire week. While I indicated my request verbally to the manager, he offered little hope of being able to accommodate my requirement; my telepathic transmission of my intention helped encourage and connect with the manager, who was unwittingly now helping change the initially impossible room availability.

I met with the conference management team and heard about the exciting speakers and itinerary. At the time, I was both consciously and overtly transmitting my intention to meet the Dalai Lama. I was also examining the flows of my communication and knew that now others were communicating with others about my intention and assisting in changing the practical realities of funding and room availability. My business brain was also aware of my financial requirements and alert to the opportunity to meet new prospective clients. While the "needs must" aspect of my predicament may have given me more focus, it was the understanding and utilisation of the communication flows which produced, as if by magic, a new client who wished to explore his awareness and asked to contract me for several hours of consultation.

I woke up the following morning and understood that I might have to move to another hotel, but the manager, communicating genuine delight and sincere disbelief, stated I could keep my room "one more night". The hotel manager wanted me to know that this would certainly be the last evening he could accommodate, because Baryshnikov was arriving with his entourage, and the hotel was seriously overbooked.

I gave the hotel manager the right to let me go and offered no resistance. I also acknowledged his help and let him know my intentions, which were to stay and to meet the Dalai Lama. I understood that HE UNDERSTOOD and he knew that I was not resisting his eviction warning, but instead communicating my empathy with his predicament. "What you resist persists" is a rhyme which I use repeatedly with communication and outcome analysis. I was NOT resisting; I was communicating and knowing there would be a positive outcome.

You won't be surprised at this point to hear that the following morning my friendly hotel manager greeted me with delight and surprise, saying, "I am so happy to tell you not to worry, I am pleased that you can stay, Ms. Brooks, through the end of the week." The manager shrugged his shoulders and laughed at the unexpected good fortune of the events. My new client, who had little cash, offered to pay for my entire week's stay on his credit card in exchange for his consultation, and my intention became closer to the outcome I both wanted and fully expected.

My first view of the Dalai Lama was with me seated in an auditorium; not the intimate encounter that I visualised, but I had faith and knowingness that my intentions would prevail. During a break in the conference I went to the powder room, where I ran into one of the speakers and an interesting scientist named Candice Pert. We laughed and communicated about the Dalai Lama and the universe and agreed to meet later over coffee. Candice Pert, sadly now deceased, was one of the proponents of Quantum Mechanics and its explanation of spirituality and connectivity. We had amazing conversations about molecules and cells and emotional reactions, which included the power of intention. Our discussions included my desire and intention to see the Dalai Lama on a more personal level, and Candice was kind to invite me to a speaker's conference later in the day.

I entered the meeting room along with about twenty speakers and acolytes of the Dalai Lama and was given a sash, which is the way one initially greets His Holiness. As an acknowledgment of your respect and your existence, you offer the sash towards the Dalai Lama, and he touches it and carries on. While less than 25 people were in attendance, I was standing in the back of the room with several people in front of me and closer to His Holiness. The conversation and topics were mesmerising, and I was thoroughly enjoying watching the participants' ability to communicate, feeling the flows.

My thoughts were: "It is so beautiful to see his Holiness interact in a non-rehearsed way with the speakers in such an intimate setting." My visualisation, however, of my meeting with the Dalai Lama was somehow more intense, and I was excited to see how that might occur. I was asked to come and sit with the speakers by one of my new friends and came closer into the room and sat down directly in front of the great man.

One of the speakers enquired: "What is telepathy and how can you know when you are getting telepathic messages?" After hearing the question, I looked up toward His Holiness and I had the thought that I had the answer to that question. After so many epiphanies and self-examinations, I knew telepathy very well. I looked at the Dalai Lama waiting for his response, and he looked at me and waited, for what seemed an eternity. The thought formed in my mind that HE knew that I knew the answer. The communication, although wordless, projected telepathically, "*Yes, you do know...*" I inhaled and felt every cell filled with His energy and thoughts. The profound sensation went straight through me and produced the thought: "You have breathed him in and now you must return his spirit to him." The amount of time this took led to an uncomfortable silence in the room, as two beings exchanged telepathic thoughts and good wishes.

The memory of that interchange with the Dalai Lama still produces in me what we call "goose-heaps" and a good deal of happiness. The only other time I have felt anything quite so profound and similar was watching my mother's soul leave her body. The connectivity we experience with another being's spirituality is always heightened by powerful intention and the expectation of an outcome. I expected my experience in meeting the Dalai Lama would be profound, like the way I anticipated the loss of my mother some years earlier. Many of us have our most profound spiritual experience when watching the departure of a loved one. I had anticipated the experience of my mother's soul being freed from her pain-ridden body, which helped produce the outcome and my ability to deal with the grief of loss.

The importance of intention and our understanding and realisation of the outcome of our intentions can be illustrated by the weeks following my meeting with the Dalai Lama. My original intention, while articulated over coffee with a friend during an innocuous conversation, had profound ramifications of which, at the time, I was only partially aware. A popular saying is "be careful what you wish for", because we normally have only a limited understanding of our intended outcomes. After returning from Germany with renewed enthusiasm for my work and quest for spiritual currency, the following days produced a flow of "connect the dot" repercussions in the wake of my profound meeting with the Dalai Lama.

Athletes call being "in the zone" that time when their endeavour feels easier and their coordination, awareness and performance is at an enhanced level. For years we have coached and trained athletes and leaders to return to what we call the "whitespace" where they can perform on an optimum level. My own "whitespace" occurred in conjunction with my return from Germany and the alignment of relationships in both personal and business areas of my life. It was quite breath-taking in hindsight.

In the space of a few days I was to meet one of my most significant long-term business partners and, through him, become affiliated to one of the most influential families in London. These "dots" of success were able to be connected because of my level of existence in the "Whitespace", which can be attributed directly to my intention and profound meeting with the Dalai Lama.

The increase in my Spiritual Currency due to my knowingness and ability to perceive and influence the outcome has led to a variety of positive outcomes in the material world, where deals and revenues are ways of keeping score. The calculation of one's spiritual currency is not as easily tallied and, like intention, requires a focus and willingness to examine which many of us find difficult to contemplate.

One area where science and literature have contributed reams of research papers is the area of energy. While the mechanical energy required to fuel our transport, homes and bodies is important, I am more interested to explore the psychic energy we receive from each other and the life-force particles which can be infused or drained by simple encounters. We all have heard the popular saying, "one bad apple can spoil the whole barrel", and realize that the analogy with friends and acquaintances is equally relevant.

Having had to travel across the Atlantic between Europe and North America many times, one indispensable requirement is my power cord adaptor. You may have made the mistake of plugging in a 110-volt appliance into a 240-volt outlet and experiencing the smoke and overcharged reaction by not using the correct adapter. People are like different electric plugs. Many times, their charges and energies may be such that we are overwhelmed and can experience a short circuit in our plugging into their energies. As our spiritual currency increases, so does our ability to ascertain the charge and energy of those we encounter. While clothes, make up, education and diplomacy can mask a variety of overcharged emotional beings, the underlying danger of connecting with these beings can be understood as our awareness and presence increases.

We require a high degree of self-mastery to modulate our own energy. The idea of duplication or the ability to adjust our own mood level to be in better communication with those around us is a benefit of increased awareness. As one's *Mobius Life Coins* increase, one's compounding Life's Capital will fund the energy and mood level required for optimum communication. The compassion and love we demonstrate to those of lower energy is important in compounding and preserving our spiritual currency.

Please access your Book of Y.O.U. CONTEMPLATION 4.
to better understand your IDENTITY

> *"Love one another and help others*
> *To rise to the higher levels,*
> *simply by pouring out love.*
> *Love is the greatest healing*
> *Energy."*

Sai Baba

4
TIME AND SPACE, PREDICTING THE FUTURE

"Death is no more than passing from one room into another. But there's a difference for me, you know. Because in that other room, I shall be able to see."

Helen Keller

"Will you look at that?" and "Do you see what I mean?" are common questions, which deal not with sight, but with understanding and perception. In a variety of languages, the sense of sight and the words used to express vision are sometimes confused and commonly used to denote knowledge. Born in the late 19th century and losing the faculties of sight and hearing at an early age, the American author and activist Helen Keller was acutely aware of her other senses, especially touch and smell. Despite not being able to hear her own words or view others verbalizing, Ms Keller was able to learn to speak by feeling the vibrations and positions of the tongue in the mouth of her friends. We will discuss the future and the perception necessary to fully experience the "now" and prepare for a better tomorrow, as contemplated in Ms Keller's above quote. The increased level of perception in highly spiritual beings is one important consideration and a significant contributor to the accumulation of Spiritual Currency.

Do you believe you can predict the future? More incredibly, do you believe that you can change your future? In fact, your very thoughts can predict your future, determine and change its outcome. The philosophical and sociological debate as to human destiny's predetermination, whether caused by external theological forces or the more mundane environmental influences, focuses on our free or pre-disposed will. If one believes that one can adapt and adjust one's attitude and belief system, then the logical conclusion is one has self-control over one's personal destiny. When one marvels at the human ability to overcome handicaps and impediments, as with the example of Helen Keller, one enhances the perception of our free will. Keller, who was a strong believer in self-determinism, demonstrated that conventional wisdom's view of her condition, as ill-fated handicaps, might be opportunities, not impediments. The ability of the human spirit to triumph against all odds is one of the important evidences of the free will of humanity.

If one believes in predestination or in an absolute power, which makes all decisions for us and determines our future, as did the ancient Greeks, then one's belief system essentially cedes control and responsibility to that pre-determination. If I were to ask you "Do you believe you are in control of your ability to decide any and all of your personal actions?", you may have your doubts. You may have engaged in actions you cannot explain, or taken decisions, as if you were pre-programmed to make those moves. And you were. The more important questions are: how were you programmed and what were those influences which determined your decision to take a certain course?

As an example, may I pose the question, "Do you have the freedom NOT to get out of bed in the morning?" You may immediately answer yes or no, based on your belief system. Or you may qualify your answer by thinking, "I have the freedom to decide, but I realise the negative consequences if I don't get out of bed and go to work; so I AM predetermined to get out of bed, based on my experience and expected outcome." Your conclusion might sound something like "I could but I wouldn't stay in bed". If that is like your thought process, then your belief system dictates your decision based on experience. The conclusions of your personal paradigm indicate the correct choice for you. We shall examine the paradigm of our personal essence and one's belief system later in this chapter, but first let us go into more depth regarding our future and the decisions, which will determine that future.

The debates surrounding free will and determinism have occupied philosophers and theologians and continue to be defined as we explore the science around neurological influences on our decision-making. The ancient Greek philosophers, such as Aristotle and to a later and greater extent Epicurus, wanted to change the public's popular belief system, which had depicted humans as puppets with strings pulled by whimsical Gods on Mt Olympus. This philosophical departure, from the concept of one's fate determined by beings in the heavens and outside of our personal control, began humanity's examination of our life force and spirituality, which continues apace.

If we examine our belief system and its evolution, as well as the evolution of philosophical theories, it is evident that over time we humans believed more and more in our personal responsibility for our actions. While theologians and philosophers have debated and debunked the Mt Olympus control of our actions, similarly, children grow up to understand that the tooth fairy does not exist. Child psychologists have identified around 7 years of age as the stage where humans exhibit the ability to understand the moral consequences of our actions and called this the "Age of Reason". In some ways, the enlightenment of humanity can be linked to the post-Aristotle belief system, which apportions responsibility and our ability to choose between right and wrong. This acceptance of responsibility is the foundation for community standards and the basis for most civil law.

In the current scientific and secular academic community, there exists a sceptical wing of thinkers with a belief system, which characterises most notions of spirituality, as being naive. These doubters of connectivity liken the concept of non-classical scientific forces as similarly immature as the belief in the tooth fairy. Richard Dawkins is one of these academic atheists, who asks, "There may be fairies at the bottom of the garden. There is no evidence for it, but you can't prove that there aren't any, so shouldn't we be agnostic with respect to fairies?" The separation of Science from Religion and the scepticism which has led to vehement and messianic atheists is beginning to swing back in a pendulum propelled by the evolving understanding and mysteries explored within the new laws of Quantum Physics. This new understanding allows for difficult concepts, which fly in the face of classical physical laws of time and space. Rumi, the 12th-century Persian poet, when contemplating this quantum "field" said, "Out beyond the ideas of right-doing and wrongdoing, there is a field I will meet you there. It's the world full of things to talk about."

The definition of "entanglement", in this new science, mathematically demonstrates the universal connection which we all have on a sub-atomic level. These new laws show that our mind and our role as observer of our universe are inextricably connected, in fact "entangled", where we alter the states we observe and can change matter by merely contemplating its existence. If human life-force is the spirit we all seek, micro-biologists have discovered, **Adenosine triphosphate (ATP)**, an energy-carrying molecule found in the cells of all living things. ATP captures chemical energy obtained from the breakdown of food molecules and releases it to fuel other cellular processes. "Entanglement" in Quantum Physics is another way of scientifically expressing the connectivity which many of us desire and intend to improve in our relationships with others and, indeed, our entire universe. When one views a model of molecules and understands that all physical matter is made up to a much greater proportion of void or empty space than particles such as neutrons, protons, electrons, etc., one realizes that our universe is well and truly empty. Many philosophers and scientists have described and studied this void in order to understand how the particles of matter can affect each other and be changed by forces which travel unseen and immeasurable across this void.

Innumerable health gurus, doctors and trainers have told us that our bodies are composed, largely, of water, and usually the warning to drink more fluids follows that observation. Similarly, our universe is composed, largely, of empty void, and yet the waves of energy including our thoughts and intentions must be emitted with goodness and kindness in order to improve our existence and increase our spiritual currency and the health of our life's capital account.

Space, on a galactic level, is fascinating, and will continue to command human interest through research and exploration. The interesting by-product of this interstellar study is the relevance to the interconnectivity in sub-atomic space, which demonstrates the importance of what Indian religions have described as Karma. We can now see the truth, through electron microscopes, in the saying "what goes around comes around", and how interconnected we truly are in a Karmic sense.

We have been programmed to glance at our wristwatch, phone or wall clock and plan our time accordingly. This classical definition of linear time with one second ticking after another is completely irrelevant in the subatomic particle behaviour described in Quantum Physics. Time and particles can stand still, and the reactions and effects have been proven to influence particle movements past and future in a non-linear way. The interesting aspect for those of us working on building our spiritual currency is the mathematically proven ability for us to alter and improve our universe, within what appears to be a finite and limited amount of time, during our current human life. The more one contemplates one's past and future actions, the more we can improve our perception and expand our consciousness and awareness of our connectivity with every particle in the universe.

Our human perception appears at first examination to be limited to our five senses. While the idea of an additional sense, intuition, is debated and scientifically tested, quantum physicists have very little scepticism in regard to the human ability to predict the future, because we are "entangled" or inextricably linked with that future and indeed all particles in the universe. Popular culture in most human societies speaks about a "sixth sense". In experiments quoted in *Psychology Today*: "The sixth sense and similar terms, like second sight and extrasensory perception (ESP), refer to perceptual experiences that transcend the usual boundaries of space and time."

While credible studies have proven human intuition exists, some sceptical scientists believe the methodology and sample sizes have been inadequate. Most of us believe in intuition because we have experienced it personally, when one of our hunches "paid off". An interesting explanation of ESP is an unconscious awareness produced by the combination of our known five senses in conjunction with our experience. Our perception based on the five known senses is always turned on even if we are not consciously tuned in. The isolation of each of our senses by such methods as blindfolding, deafening ear coverage, nose plugs, etc., invariably allows us to focus and become more aware of our non-impaired senses. No doubt we can improve our sensory perception through a variety of exercises and, or, mechanical means such as eyeglasses and hearing aids. Our ability to absorb and collate information on an unconscious level far exceeds our conscious realisation of those inputs.

The phenomenon of "déjà vu" can be explained due to our unconscious recognition of a similar arrangement of sensory inputs from past events. This feeling of having been "there" before may be true and our conscious mind does not remember when we had been "there", or it may be a trick, because of the sensory similarities which our sub-conscious mind is attempting to bring to conscious recognition. The sensory connections and storage of information in our brain's memory may produce this feeling of intuition, when in fact it is just an unconscious awareness which triggers our recognition or prediction of outcomes. In Quantum theory, the connection of all particles in the universe has been explained, if not completely understood, and can be used to further understand the possibilities of psychic experiences.

We know and readily admit our mind's eye can play tricks on us. We enjoy illusions, whether optical or physical, because they illustrate that each of our senses is far from perfect and less than acute. The fact that our sense of smell is used much less now than our hunting and gathering ancestors, who relied on this sense to find food and avoid danger, is one illustration of how little we use the senses we do have. That Helen Keller could learn to speak without ever seeing or hearing language or her own words, by using her fingertips in her highly developed sense of touch, demonstrates how one can expand the use of our normal senses. The importance of staying tuned in to our perceptions using meditation and mental agility techniques will enhance the awareness of our place in the universe.

One other important aspect of time and space is the examination of how our perceptions and dreams can be made into reality or, conversely, inhibit our becoming more spiritual. Science can distinguish between the brain and mind but has difficulty in describing exactly where one begins and the other ends. If we examine our intentions and compare them to our outcomes or results, we can see how our belief system is increasing or detracting from our spiritual currency.

Please turn to CONTEMPLATION 6. Book of Y.O.U. to examine your belief system.

Modern determinist philosophers, while examining genetic and environmental influences on our decision-making process, have embraced the notion of blame and guilt when the correct or logical decision is not made. We come to blame ourselves to a greater or lesser degree based on our belief paradigm. The healthiest way to increase our life's capital is by examining our belief system, "out-creating" and evolving our understanding of our spirituality and decision-making. This is not blame and guilt but taking responsibility for our future and our spirituality.

The increase of our perception while engaging our senses is more importantly influenced by our intention or spirit. Helen Keller had far fewer sensory abilities than most of us, yet her spirit was rich, and her results, which included such diverse accomplishments as the development of the American Foundation for the Blind and helping to obtain the right to vote for women in the US, attest to her robust belief system. Keller was quoted as saying, "…character cannot be developed in ease and quiet. Only through experience of trial and suffering can the soul be strengthened, ambition inspired, and success achieved."

If one diagrams a common belief system, it begins with the "ambition" or dreams each of us hold in our heart, which may be more or less achievable based on our experience and which has been trapped or released from our previous belief system. We jealously guard and protect our belief system and find it difficult to let go, unless we have a paradigm crash, which violently destroys our homeostatic balance. This balance is normal in all humans and is typically upset by SPIRITUALLY sapping events, which may include heartbreak, loss of love or loved ones, illness, change of home or jobs among other traumatic occurences. One of the most salient aspects of our belief system is the realisation that our "intentions have no intelligence". Let me say that again: INTENTIONS HAVE NO INTELLIGENCE. This motto is more than just the popular saying, "Be careful what you wish for", but is related, in so far as most of us are not in tune with the relationship and, indeed, recursive nature of the four columns of our belief paradigm.

These four concepts form the basis for the foundation of our belief structure, which floats upon our normally unintelligent dreams. This paradigm structure is not only inter-connected like any building with four columns but also dynamically interactive. The four elements of a belief system can be described as follows – throughout the remainder of the Chapter these four columns will be highlighted in **BOLD CAPITALS**.

1. ENVISION is the creation, actually or in our mind, of a mock-up of what our ambition looks like. This first column is sometimes called modelling.

2. STRATEGY is the second column which is logically created to build or achieve our visualisation. An accurate model will help in detailing our "STRATEGY", and a well-conceived plan will have a greater chance of achieving the intended model.

3. IMPLEMENT is the execution of our "'strategy'" as modelled when we "envision" our new paradigm. Our efficiency in implementation is directly related to the intelligence of our plan and the accuracy of our model.

4. OUTCOME or result is the fourth and last column which is produced by our accurately modelled and well-planned implementation of our intention. Depending on the strength and purpose of each corner, the other corners will benefit, and the speed and efficacy of our paradigm will improve in comparison to our former belief system.

Rather than an abstract structure, let us examine a real-life paradigm. A frequent example can be found in the frequent beliefs that love and a loving relationship are desirable and possible. Our INTENTION to find a romantic partner is an aspiration and quite normal dream. The INTENTION (to have a romance) does not, for most of us, come with health warnings and an in-depth understanding of the possible and best OUTCOMES. If our paradigm, as with most young

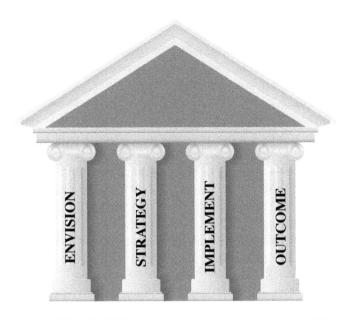

lovers, **ENVISIONS** a romantic relationship and fulfilling partner as the best and most plausible.

OUTCOME: we may have skipped the important columns of modelling and **PLANNING** our relationship. Most romantic INTENTIONS are the least intelligent, especially when fuelled by hormonal urges or obscured by the intoxication of excitement and possibly outside chemical influences. The truth of that observation was brought to my attention on the back of a T-shirt which stated, "God made alcohol so ugly people could have sex." Young innocent lovers may have their MODEL based on some Hollywood image of beauty and happiness. The other columns, which incorporate a **STRATEGY** and **IMPLEMENTATION** of a nurturing and co-creative relationship, are many times ignored, weakening the paradigm and initiating the structural flaws, which will precipitate the paradigm crash.

While desire and an articulation of our INTENTION are important first steps in successful outcomes, the promotion of our intention does not automatically make it intelligent. The intelligence comes with perceiving and testing our model while constantly breaking and improving our structure. This is how good performers who achieve successful **OUTCOMES** can make their last peak performance the platform or base for the next higher achievement. Many relationship advisors who grasp the importance of our belief paradigm will caution that relationships can never be static but only be improving or deteriorating. This duality is also true of belief systems, which are constantly crashing or being tweaked and improved.

If we follow a young woman's first romantic paradigm, it may illustrate how one's belief system can evolve. A young woman has the INTENTION to have a family. Her MODEL is based on her parents who have successfully raised several children and appear to be relatively happy. This young woman's DREAM is rather nebulous, but she knows that she is attractive to young men and finds the idea of passionate love exciting.

Her MODEL is not only limited by her personal experience but doesn't contemplate problems which were few and shielded from her view by parents who were very private in their own relationship. She **ENVISIONS** dating, engagement, wedding and children with the expected RESULT of a happy family, where her partner is a good provider and father to her children. Her STRATEGY is focused on the identification, seduction and acquisition of a partner and lacks important considerations of how to anticipate and handle problems. She studies and discusses with other girls the art of seduction, including dress, manners and flirting, but has little thought for how the relationship might evolve or what stress may inhibit the IMPLEMENTATION of her **STRATEGY**. The **OUTCOME** of a happy family and children is partially achieved, but the drudgery of being a mother and giving up her career, coupled with her husband's loss of job, create a PARADIGM CRASH. I am called to counsel the young mother in reassessing her INTENTIONS and belief system.

We begin by studying the inadequacies of the previous paradigm and the young woman redefines her dream and builds on her previous belief system. Her INTENTION of a producing a happy family and loving relationship is no more intelligent but has evolved in enhancing her perception of the importance and interrelation of the four columns which underpin her new belief system. Her MODEL of a happy relationship includes many more co-creative and partner-oriented activities, which draws heavily on her spiritual currency. Our plan includes aspects of healthier mental and physical activities such as meditation, nutrition and yoga. The written evidence of our well-conceived belief system includes a check-up where the strategy can be adjusted to handle unforeseen events without a major paradigm crash and possible spiritual bankruptcy. It is not enough to have an INTENTION or say, "I really want something", without understanding the paradigm columns, which can make your dreams a reality.

One of the problems with most belief systems is they are embedded in our psyche and are seldom recognized or studied. These paradigms just exist and persist unless we take the time to understand the mantras and self-hypnotic suggestions we constantly give ourselves. The separation and silencing of our inner dialogue through meditation is one way to review our belief system. Like the difficulty of reading a book while simultaneously listening to a talk show on radio, our brain is unable to focus but subconsciously takes the input into our psyche. Our conscious mind ebbs and flows, alternating from perceiving the book to listening to the voice on the radio. If we silence the noise of our inner voice and isolate one area of our belief system, the concentration will allow us to improve and tweak the habits and understandings we have developed over time. One benefit of this introspection is to discover how our paradigm may be interfering with the accumulation of spiritual currency.

When a competitive tennis player tracks and reads the statistics of his performance, he improves his personal perception of areas of weakness in his game. Invariably the athlete will find one stroke or area of his game which needs work. For example, the player may request his instructor to help him work on his backhand in his next practice session. The competitor understands that he has hit fewer winners and has lost more points on that side of his game and seeks to improve his ability by drilling that particular stroke. The coach hits ball after ball to the same area, tweaking the aspects of racquet position, knee bend, body turn and footwork. This is called "grooving your swing" in tennis parlance, but in fact is re-grooving or improving the entire game on the backhand side. We have an exercise, which combines meditation, concentration and isolation of various key aspects of our existence. The tennis player, by improving one aspect of his game, improves his entire game. When it comes to life, changing our belief system without isolating aspects of our operating system becomes a psychological impossibility which leads to the trauma of a paradigm crash. By reading this book and exploring your spirituality, you are taking an important step which will increase your Life's Capital account. This self-examination can decrease, and in some cases eliminate, paradigm crashes or those events which completely upset our homeostatic balance.

Most of my clients and friends focus on one area of their paradigm which they recognise is limiting their spiritual currency, but they may do this without the statistics or information to make that perception a reality. We usually seek help when we have a problem or paradigm crash. The normal events of physical sickness, including mental and spiritual illness, are the main reasons we look for outside assistance. In the next chapter, we will explore WELLNESS, which is a concept that is seldom examined in holistic terms. The almost imperceptible changes to our diet, sleep, exercise and meditation can combine to upset our health and well-being. Much like the tennis player who ignores or fails to study his performance statistics, our paradigm examinations can be ignored, and this data avoidance results in loss. The tennis player may focus on percentages of forehand, backhand, service, return of serve, etc., studying where his game is weakest and strongest. By studying our past statistics, we can improve our future performance.

We now can examine our paradigm and ask ourselves, preferably by writing, "What are our top three DREAMS or INTENTIONS?" You may wonder, "Why only three?" and my answer would be: whatever you think is your most important goal may change by the mere examination of the INTENTION. What we carry around as our most important dreams may be whimsical when compared and contrasted to each other.

A wise man once said that "a goal without a written plan, which includes the time and resources required to **IMPLEMENT,** is just wishful thinking." Philosophers and intellectuals have written about "good intentions" and the inherent dangers such as St Bernard of Clairvaux, who supposedly wrote in the 12th century, "*L'enfer est plein de bonnes volontés et désirs*" ("hell is full of good wishes and desires"). This admonition has evolved into the popular saying, "The road to Hell is paved with good intentions." After writing down our prioritized top three intentions, we have already improved our chances of winning a successful **OUTCOME.**

We began this chapter by examining human perception and how it relates to our belief systems. The good news is our spiritual currency is growing along with our increased perception of our belief systems, as we isolate and contemplate the interrelationships of the paradigm dynamic. The question of predicting our future becomes more perceivable as the chances for positive **OUTCOMES** improves by **IMPLEMENTATION** of our **STRATEGY.** Can we predict the future and influence our destiny? The answer is a most definite YES, if we understand and constantly improve the personal paradigm of our belief system.

One of the most common complaints is: "I do not have enough time." Most of my clients, when asked to list what they want more of, usually prioritise "time" as one of their most important necessities. If we are fatalistic, we think, unimaginable forces determine our life span. Our fatalistic inclinations may not include Greek gods on Mt Olympus, but equally remote and immutable determinations. Most languages on earth have some concept of "what is written" and when one's "time is up" as a concept of limited and scarily unpredictable temporal existence.

As we contemplate time, it may occur to you, as with many of my clients, that there is so much to do and so little time. It is a human condition to feel that one's day and indeed one's life is all too brief. The good news is, no matter how brief our life may be, the more we are interconnected with our present, past and future, the more our ability to influence and grow our spiritual currency will become. If we examine historic figures, it is evident that much can be accomplished in a short time. This is no better evidence than the brief life of Alexander the Great, who ruled for only 13 years (336–323 BC) after inheriting the throne and army of Macedon at the young age of 20. No doubt, the advantages of an education by Aristotle and training with an ambitious and militarily skilled father increased Alexander's chances for success. In just over a decade, Alexander's armies were able to conquer Egypt, Persia and most of Asia.

It would be interesting to understand Alexander's belief system, which obviously included an insatiable ambition for conquest, but he was also strong on **ENVISION** and **STRATEGY** and had the military skills of **IMPLEMENTATION** in order to achieve his victorious **OUTCOMES**. Alexander the Great had a belief system which in a very brief time allowed him to wage military campaigns and significantly influence various cultures, and which appears even more remarkable when compared with modern monarchs and dictators. When one contemplates the lengthy dictatorships of Saddam Hussein, Hosni Mubarak and Muammar al Gaddafi, who each ruled a small part of the territories of Alexander's empires, it is clear that "time" in office is NOT the most significant factor in successful belief systems. Alexander died with many unfinished plans, but it is difficult to contemplate a leader who accomplished more in such a short period of existence. Lincoln said, "The best thing about the future is that it comes one day at a time." We all have an equal amount of time each day and that understanding must be incorporated within our belief system in order to maximise our **OUTCOMES**.

When our universe is viewed on a molecular level, the time it takes to accomplish collisions of particles with wondrous combinations and alterations is so brief as to be non-existent. When viewed in classical, linear time, our current physical life can appear not only brief but inconsequential. We expand our efficient use of time when we incorporate in our belief system our own future and past and that of humanity and our universe. Time becomes an element of our **STRATEGY**, and its judicious use through efficient **IMPLEMENTATION** predicts successful **OUTCOMES**. If our future is to be enjoyable, then our belief system must function to adapt and orient our use of time and space for maximum efficiency. While organization and prioritization are concepts typically explored in any system which attempts to give us more time, the understanding of the interrelation of our belief system is more important than time-saving tips. It is that interrelation of the important elements of our paradigm that gains time through constant feedback, leading to greater efficiency.

We have all had those moments when our routine is interrupted by an unexpected event. Normally, reliable outcomes based on experience and repetition of our daily routine can make these upsets an even greater shock to our belief system. If you have a normal repetitive commute, as most urban dwellers today, the upset of traffic and mass-transit interruptions can be very disconcerting, especially when they are unexpected and unusual. Studies have shown that the emotional anger experienced in "road rage" is increased in proportion to the surprise of a sudden traffic tailback and less related to the amount of delay caused in our JOURNEY.

In our discussion, we have examined time, space and the future and found that relativity in these concepts is an evolving science. The more important aspects of our future are how we adjust our paradigms and evolve our belief systems. It is the examination and the feedback we perceive which determines our future. The great American composer Leonard Bernstein spoke to the urgency and time required for greatness, and although he only mentions "two things… needed", his music belies the belief system which harmonised the four elements of **ENVISION**, **STRATEGY**, **IMPLEMENT, producing successful concert OUTCOMES**.

> *"To achieve great things, two things are needed; a plan, and not quite enough time."*
>
> *Leonard Bernstein*

5
CREATIVITY AND CONSCIOUSNESS

As one seeks to compound one's Life's Capital, the undeniable relationship between Creativity and Consciousness can reveal the importance of exploring our universal connectivity. While business seeks to connect to its clients and maintain a connection between its employees, the following chapter provides a real-world scenario which demonstrates how awareness and perspective can compound our Spiritual Currency through increased consciousness.

You may not have your *own* business, but your household *is* a business with a budget, income, expenses, intentions and outcomes. While this chapter evolved from my commercial practice, it is illustrative of how to apply the Spiritual Currency to the coin of the realm.

Every company struggles to embrace the three primary requirements which contribute to their short- and long-term success:

- to inspire innovation,
- to encourage creativity and
- to increase their employees' consciousness.

In our corporate consultancy practice, Whitespace defines "to innovate" not only, as the *Oxford Dictionary* suggests, to "*introduce something new, especially a product*", but more broadly as:

"Make changes in something established, especially by introducing new methods, ideas or products."

The most prolific inventors would be stymied if they were bound by a strict definition of innovation, such as producing something completely new. In fact, they understand and never shy away from the counter-intuitive process of "reinventing the wheel", which leads to the biggest productivity gains.

Imagine the thousands of inventive engineers throughout the history of wheel development, who made incremental innovations, taking the rough-hewn round rock wheels popularised in the *Flintstones* cartoons and found lighter, stronger, rounder, and more durable materials and processes to evolve and adapt this basic transportation component. Modern F1 cars' wheels can be changed in less than 15 seconds and endure speeds in excess of 200 miles per hour, with loads exceeding five tons. These racing wheels are constantly being "re-invented" in order to maximise performance and it is the innovation, inspired by F1 competition, which trickles down to make our road cars safer, smoother and more economical. The best engineers employed by these F1 racing teams are incremental innovators, constantly tweaking materials and processes while spending millions on research and testing in order to discover the minute changes, which may give them a competitive advantage.

University of Exeter Professor John Bessant teaches a course called Innovation and Entrepreneurship. The professor further expands the definition of innovation for his students to include the concept of "creating value from ideas". The ultimate test for any business is the conversion of ideas into a viable commercial proposition, and the professor emphasises the long and arduous road of this process of innovation. When asked what the key ingredients for business innovation are, Professor Besant responded with the following paraphrased bullet points:

- An organisational strategy or roadmap identifying the value and purpose of innovation;
- An atmosphere which promotes idea creation and collaboration between the innovators;
- A safe environment which permits failure and encourages experimentation;
- A managed portfolio of innovation which mixes long-term and short-term as well as high-risk and low-risk innovations;
- Time and patience which allows the corporate strategy and the innovators to adapt to the market requirements.

An important consideration for organisations wishing to create valuable ideas is the communication of the firm intention to foment innovation. All too often in our experience, corporations isolate the innovators and, indeed, the innovation strategy from their non-technical departments, clients and competitors. Most corporate directors profess to communicate strategy and promote innovation but miss out on the preliminary step: the emotional commitment to have the decisive intention to inspire innovation. It is a corporate mindset which radiates creativity that attracts innovators and promotes inspiration.

One of the world's most successful creative companies is indubitably Google, which has its own Creative Lab. In its unique application for 5 paid positions, they announce they are looking for candidates, who will work, *"with talented folks who make things that matter"*, again we see the link between innovation, teamwork and the concept of value. Google is proud of its reputation to create and, from top to bottom, the corporate mindset is proudly innovative. Steve Vranakis, the former Google Creative Lab Executive Creative Director, speaks to that corporate mindset:

"When we talk about magic, we talk about the emotional connection you are going to make to something and the benefit

and value it's going to bring you. From a brand perspective, our whole thing is about being the stage and our users being the stars."

Creative "types" conjure up images of thick spectacles, staring at multiple computer screens, and being "nerds" or socially awkward. The reality is the best innovators enjoy the collaboration and idea interchange with their colleagues, clients and indeed competitors. Connectivity works on the emotional requirements of creativity and builds confidence. Creativity requires a mental resilience toward failure and a dogged determination to develop one's own story. Rumi, said it well: *"Don't be satisfied with stories, how things have gone with others. Unfold your own myth."* The following anecdote illustrates how to create your own story.

Whitespace Business Dynamics was recently contracted by a South London-based SME to help raise the consciousness of one of their "fast-tracked" female directors, *Martha*. The Chairman and CEO of this SME requested us to help *Martha* break out of the boardroom paradigms and inspire her creativity. *Martha* related that, all too often, when she had a good idea the "suits" would dismiss her suggestions as too emotional or not economically feasible. Whitespace consultants analysed a typical boardroom problem and helped *Martha* discover a creative and innovative solution.

Martha's company is located in a 20-storey home office building with several floors sublet to other renters, which provided flexibility and important revenue to the SME. The problem presented to the Monday-morning directors' meeting was described as a "continual and increasing complaint that the 8 lifts which serviced the building were too slow and causing waiting times of 4 to 11 minutes during peak usage". The tenants were threatening breaking rental contracts and even legal remediation. The two most popular solutions to the problem, proposed by senior male directors, included a new control programme and lift segregation to dedicated floors which promised to reduce waiting times by 20% and cost one million pounds. The second proposed solution would build two additional lifts and incur over two million pounds of capital expenditure while lowering waiting times by an estimated 40%. The two solutions were adamantly supported in a testosterone-fuelled head-butting debate by their respective directors. The CEO asked *Martha* and the others to come up with some ideas for the next Monday meeting, when a decision would be made.

Whitespace challenged *Martha* to view the problem from three different perspectives:

1. A remote helicopter view, as if *Martha* was watching the crowded lift lobby from above.
2. A focused internal view; how *Martha* personally felt while standing waiting for the lift at a peak time.
3. An imaginative and empathetic exploration of the feelings of the frustrated tenants.

In the first remote viewing perspective, *Martha* related that she could see the lift lobby filling up and the waiting crowd exchanging pleasantries in small groups which soon disintegrated into a vocal and angry gang of frustrated tenants. *Martha* noticed how the men would fidget with their suits and phones and frequently check their watches. The women also would check their phones but often fuss with their hair or make-up. In *Martha's* mind's eye, they appeared bored.

When *Martha* reviewed her personal feelings, she discovered that she had made it a habit to arrive early and leave late in order to avoid the 9 a.m. and 5 p.m. rush period. The recognition by *Martha* that she hadn't really experienced the problem to the same degree as the tenants helped her realise why she hadn't been able to create a solution. She needed to be *present* to fuel her creativity.

In the third perspective, *Martha* was asked to empathise with the tenants and feel their frustration. This collaborative exercise is analogous to the prerequisite for successful innovation, which is to listen and understand what the client wants.

Martha developed three solutions which she confidently proposed at the next Monday meeting:

1. Redecorate the lift lobby with mirrors, so the waiting workers could check their "look".
2. Install 4 television monitors showing headline news, giving information and further distraction.
3. Institute an alternative workday schedule for the home office employees, changing 9 to 5 to an easy to remember 8:30 a.m. to 4:30 p.m. on even-numbered calendar days and 9:30 a.m. to 5:30 p.m. on odd-numbered calendar days; reducing rush-hour concentration significantly.

Total cost for *Martha's* innovative solutions was less than one hundred thousand pounds. The CEO was impressed with the creativity brought to the solutions and the proposal was adopted unanimously. Complaints about waiting times disappeared.

The popular admonition "Think outside of the box" is further evidence of what is required to inspire creativity and foment innovation. We are often asked to change mindsets, those preconceived notions which become a corporate paradigm. A simple exercise illustrates how we are constricted by our perspectives and suffer from the psychological affliction of *habituation*.

Habituation is defined by our friends at the *Oxford Dictionary* as "*the diminishing of an innate response to a frequently repeated stimulus*". In our world of standardisation, we fail to notice things that may have once been fascinating during our childhood. To demonstrate the mind's propensity to *habituate,* Whitespace will ask a group of our executive clients, "How many corners are there in this room?" Overwhelmingly our habituated participants respond, "FOUR". Possibly having to sit in a *corner* for misbehaviour during our youth, combined with the ubiquitous GPS warnings to turn right or left at the next *corner*, contributes to the habituation of our two-dimensional perspective. When Whitespace consultants point out that there are eight corners, our habituation is removed to reveal a three-dimensional space. We perceive the majority of our information from screens and printed words and maps and diagrams... all in two dimensions. Our mind can standardise and simplify our perception by eliminating the less used third dimension.

To "think outside of the box" one must first perceive the box and expand the perspective. Creativity and innovation are inextricably linked to the magic one experiences as a child. Picasso said, "Every child is an artist, the problem is to remain an artist once we grow up." Our mind has had years of working to simplify our existence by habituating our perceptions. The importance of pushing out our view to all corners of the room, both literally and figuratively, is basic to creativity.

The human ego and habituated mind tend to see all problems from the logical and simplified perspective of, *what's in front of me and what's behind me?* The realisation of our ego-centred view allows our expanded consciousness to include the perceptions of *what's above me and what's below me?* It takes further self-awareness to realise the importance of *what's inside me and how does that make me feel?* And with truly expanded consciousness we can evolve our perception to understand the importance of *how does this make others feel?* The late and great Steve Jobs encouraged his engineers to perceive how the clients would feel when using the Apple products. Watching his young daughter point to images on her computer would inspire Jobs to create the technology of touch screens, which have become a global phenomenon.

We are constantly reminded of the inextricable links between these concepts and the urgency for all of us to experience the fulfilment and satisfaction of an expanded self-awareness. The beauty in repetition of conventional wisdom is that it is easy to remember even when turned on its head. The artful aspect of expanded consciousness is to constantly strive to "reinvent the wheel" and "to think outside of the box".

> *"Don't let the noise of others' opinions drown out your own inner voice."*
>
> *Steve Jobs, Stanford University commencement speech, 2005*

6.
INTENTION-ARTIFICIAL INTELLIGENCE AND DECISION-MAKING

"Imagination is not only the uniquely human capacity to envision that which is not and, therefore, the foundation of all invention and innovation. In its arguably most transformative and revelatory capacity, it is the power that enables us to empathize with humans whose experiences we have never shared."

J.K. Rowling

As we explore our human intelligence, mindset and indeed intention, it is important to recognise the practical applications of our increasing Spiritual Currency. In my consultations with both individuals and companies I find the challenges are similar. How we can incorporate the latest artificial intelligence and technological advances to foment creativity and innovation is paramount to the success of our personal business interests. The questions discussed in this chapter will include, why a business should innovate? And how to make wise choices using the latest technological advances in artificial intelligence? If your life does not include a business orientation, nonetheless, you may wish to read this chapter to understand how the pursuit of Spiritual Currency can be applied in pursuit of one of the basic instincts which distinguishes humans from other animals: that is the urge to innovate.

WHY INNOVATE? WHAT DOES IT REALLY MEAN?

If you take as a given that innovation is necessary for any business and, indeed, society to advance and flourish, then you may be reading this book to find an edge in your quest to improve your company by improving yourself. If, however, you are an inventor, then you may *not* have the requisite mindset to be an innovator. Common wisdom would argue that if one can invent something then, surely, one is automatically an innovator. The confusion begins when one reviews the popular definitions for the noun "innovation". Merriam-Webster Dictionary offers these definitions: 1. *The introduction of something new. 2. A new method, idea or device.*

When one explores other knowledge sources such as Wikipedia, they begin with the same definition for innovation as "*something new*" but go on to expand the idea by stating "*innovation takes place through the provision of more effective products, processes... that are made available to markets, governments and society*". If, however, the inventor who builds a *better* mousetrap does not require a *brand-new* mousetrap and the inventor is able to commercialise and positively affect society with his mousetrap, then that inventor is truly an innovator. Innovations are thus incremental improvements which satisfy our clients' needs and demands rather than just something new or different.

The futurist and author Jacob Morgan gives a more easily understood example, which is important if you and your company want to innovate. He asks, "Is Google Glass an invention or an innovation?" And offers in contrast: "Is the Apple iPhone an innovation or an invention?" This is not just a discussion of semantics but goes to the core of the dilemma. If the invention of Google Glass, while novel and definitionally appearing to be an innovation, remains an oddity with little commercial acceptance or demand, then the invention of Google Glass, he argues, is *not* an innovation. The iPhone, Morgan states, is "both new and has had a profound influence in the way we communicate, store and access data", which makes it truly an innovation. It is, as Wikipedia offers, "the more effective" inventions which result in an innovation and the inventor and his company being classified as an innovator.

At a recent social gathering I was asked: "What are you working on?", and I replied, "We are helping a business foment innovation." My friend immediately asked, "What have they invented?" My reply was: "They have invented a new intention, and indeed, a new mindset." I wasn't being glib or enigmatic, but have found that the stated intention to innovate, which includes the goal of delivering something new or at least better and the mindset to commercialise the output of their work, is the basic requisite for any company to be considered truly innovative.

"INTENTIONS HAVE NO INTELLIGENCE"

Unfortunately, the word *new* and the promise of innovation has become ubiquitous in our lives as any visit to the supermarket will attest. It is obvious in every aisle of our shopping that *new* and *improved* can apply to everything from apples to zucchinis. All too often, leaders of business have a mindset which says, "innovation is just some business school hype or marketing speak." The scepticism surrounding innovation is that it has little relevance to the day-to-day operation of the company. We strongly suggest the company "vision" or "mission statement", which is necessarily a broad generalisation to be delivered over a long period, should include the *intelligent intention* to innovate. The company's long view must be accompanied by the short-term deliverable projects, which will become commercially viable and make a difference to their clients and shareholders.

The following diagram demonstrates how the importance

of long- and short-term goals relate to a company's ability to innovate. We would argue that in all three areas of Mission, Strategic Goals and Operating Objectives there must be a stated, and determined, intention to innovate; not lip service, but a firm and communicated intention; not just a hope but an intelligent intention.

The requirement for specific and short-term projects to produce commercial success is the test, which will prove whether the new product or process is truly innovative.

Ever since Peter Drucker argued in the Harvard Business Review in 1996 that "Innovation is the specific function of entrepreneurship", business consultancies have been attempting to assist companies to change their mindset. Drucker's premise instructs companies to promote "wealth-producing resources" as a fundamental goal for their employees. As the twenty-first century continues to make great advances in artificial intelligence, it appears that business leaders may now be hoping that technology will provide these much sought-after resources and innovations.

WILL ARTIFICIAL INTELLIGENCE ASSIST INNOVATION?

Arvind Krishna, CEO of IBM says, "Faced with a constant onslaught of data, we needed a new type of system that learns and adapts, and we now have that with Artificial Intelligence (AI)." Krishna further states, regarding the use of AI in business innovation, "What was deemed impossible a few years ago is not only becoming possible, it's very quickly becoming necessary and expected."

In just the last decade AI has exploded because of the combination of big data with powerful graphics processing units (GPUs), which has benefited from employing the well-known model of Deep Learning. We all remember the stories of Deep Blue which was programmed by the forefathers of IBM Research back in the 20th century and which culminated in a competition with the Russian Chess Master Gary Kasparov in 1996. It was IBM's Deep Learning which allowed the computer to analyse the millions of chess moves and which revealed artificial intelligence as one of the most important technologies to be developed into the 21st century.

It is this Deep Learning popularised by Deep Blue which will be educated by Deep Reasoning in order to create a new technology, enabling machines to conduct unsupervised learning. It is the human brain function of unsupervised

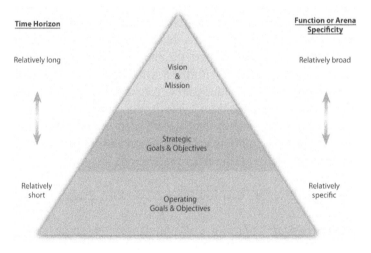

learning which continues to baffle the technologists. IBM Research is attempting to make machines curious and to seek answers. These machines will indeed produce new questions, as they learn from each other, but this is proving far more difficult than the much-discussed language and image recognition applications.

The emotional side of facial recognition, for example, and the reasoning which humans develop from a young age, is much more difficult for Deep Learning to grasp. Computer scientists are working with neuroscientists and psychiatrists to help the advanced computer facial recognition of emotional indications. Dr Fei Fei, Professor of Computer Science at

Stanford University says AI image recognition struggles to identify and interpret emotions; the computer's cognition is like the human condition classified as *Alexithymia*. This is a condition which inhibits some humans from both expressing and recognising emotions, often accompanying autism and other psychological disorders. IBM research, however, has made great strides in image recognition which is helping identify and diagnose a variety of illnesses and pathologies.

One example of AI image recognition is the computer application which assists the clinician in recognising melanoma lesions on human skin. While a clinician may be confident in recognising a certain type of lesion within a predominant racial skin colour, they dramatically increase their diagnostic ability with the AI database. The computer can compare, select and identify from a much greater range of images and skin tones and alert the doctor to possible areas of concern from patients they are not accustomed to treating. The use of AI in pathological recognition and diagnosis meets the societal impact criteria for innovation.

ARTIFICIAL INTELLIGENCE AND DECISIONS

Hollywood and science-fiction authors may sensationalise the possibilities for unethical or humanity threatening decisions from artificial intelligence; however, most computer scientists find this dystopian vision to be less than probable. The fascination with the human brain and the sensory inputs which we take for granted underlines the complexity and difficulty in using artificial intelligence to reason. The intersection of Deep Learning with Deep Reasoning will produce innovative products and help business leaders make better and more informed decisions.

Aya Soffer, IBM Director of AI and Cognitive Analytics Research says, "Computers don't have common sense." Humans grow up "understanding gravity" and inertia and the physical properties which allow us to function. A simple example of "objects staying where they are put", or moving, if influenced by wind or vibration or gravity, is extremely complex for A.I to comprehend at the mathematical level. It is human common sense, which is a mysterious combination of learned and inherent genetic wisdom, that is difficult for computer models to simulate and understand.

Our life experience may, however, make common-sense decisions difficult. One popular test of common sense, which is easily passed by 4- and 5-year-olds, is almost always failed by adult participants. It starts with the simple question of "How do you put a giraffe in a refrigerator?" Most adults struggle, consider size and cutting up pieces, etc., while the child answers, "You open the door and put in the giraffe and close the door." The test continues with, "How do you put an elephant in the refrigerator?" Adults again consider size and possibilities, animal cruelty and many permutations, while children, who learn and remember with greater focus on short-term memory, answer correctly, "You open the refrigerator and take out the giraffe and put in the elephant." While humorous, the quiz does illustrate how complicated and layered our decision-making process can become after years of apparently logical conclusions.

If the confluence of Deep Reasoning with Deep Learning can assist the innovator with decision-making, then it stands to reason that more useful inventions and applications will be made available. If machine learning struggles with common sense and emotional components, it is important to understand the human decision-making process. It is correct decision-making which is critical for the creative employees and inventors to produce a viable product. Artificial intelligence is credited with the image and voice recognition which has produced innovative products like Amazon's Alexa and Apple's iPhone. The retrieval of libraries of information now resident on our smartphone is another example of machines assisting humans in decision-making. The basic human cognitive function is now being studied using Quantum

Theory, which will improve the Deep Reasoning technology and accelerate the human decision-making process.

QUANTUM COGNITION

While computers are learning from the human capacity to increase the machine's perceptive abilities, the world of Quantum Theory is helping humans understand their own mental faculties. Artificial intelligence can recognise faces and pathologies and can understand voice and a variety of human speech and languages, but it is the nuance of human perception which continues to be difficult. We can teach a computer to see and perceive a square, but human vision can see and intuitively perceive three dimensions, as in the cube below, although it is obviously drawn in only two dimensions. Humans can see both the facial profiles, as well as the urn, in the second image below, and decide contextually which image is the more applicable. The human mind is being studied to understand what allows us to have these simultaneously efficient perceptions and intuitions.

The human brain is often said to rely on intuition or "gut" reactions, and this Quantum Cognition is being understood on a molecular and chemical level. The mind, however, is not the brain and the distinctions are important, if innovators are to develop the correct mindset and an accurate decision-making process. Daniel Siegel, UCLA psychiatrist and author, defines the mind and distinguishes it from the brain as follows. "The mind is an embodied and relational process in relationship to other minds, that regulates the flow of energy and information in the whole ecosystem." He further explained, "Your mind is listening as I am sharing thoughts and those thoughts are converted into electrical impulses."

The further development of artificial intelligence will increasingly understand the human mind's electrical impulses and become part of, and possibly linked directly to, the mind's ecosystem. A variety of recent studies have defined these mental information flows throughout the human nervous system. So, the idea of an emotionally "heavy heart" or a "gut feeling" is a scientifically correct way to map our human thought process. If you are an inventor and an aspiring innovator, the important take-away from these discoveries is that one should trust their instincts and commit to decisions. Commitment to your invention and the passion to procure the investment funding is key to the commercial success of your ideas.

DECISIONS AND CHOICES

Deep Learning can provide the data to help test your inventive theories and machine intelligence can be a key component of the team you assemble to produce your innovation. Different academic disciplines, including psychiatry, neurobiology, psychology and even philosophy, are studying how we make choices and decide. Because of the human emotional component to our thought process, the lack of emotion of deep learning and deep reasoning provided by artificial intelligence can produce more objective conclusions, untainted by preconceived notions and human foibles. The importance of choice has been studied for thousands of years and the mathematician and discoverer of the geometrical theorem which carries his name said:

"Choices are the hinges of destiny."
            Pythagoras (570 BC–495 BC), Greek philosopher

If your destiny is to be an innovator and contribute to an innovative enterprise then your decision-making and the choices required will be fundamental to your success. We are often asked for an easy process to increase one's probability of reaching the correct conclusion. Artificial intelligence can help in the information and analysis of the data to form an informed decision. Seeking the programmes which can test your theories in a time and economically efficient manner will help your project realise its objective. Our Whitespace team offers this innovative process, which describes the important components, leading to inspired decisions...

Inspired decisions follow the process encapsulated with the acronym RED-OP:

R. *retrieve* all the data and pertinent information available (AI will help).

E. *evaluate* the factors and outcomes (AI can test your probable outcomes).

D. *deliberate* and follow your intuition, your heart and indeed your gut.

O. *opt* for the best solution by the deadline which you have set. Time is definitely money.

P. *passionately commit* to your decision and communicate your firm intention to your team.

EXECUTIVE SUMMARY AND CONCLUSION

The definition of innovation must include the commercial viability of the product, process or service, and just being new, or better, is not enough to achieve innovation. In order to move an idea or desire to produce an innovation, the firm intention, communicated to the entire organisation, and indeed potential clients, is a fundamental requirement for success. While the intention to innovate is often found in long-term mission statements, it is even more important in the short-term, time-constrained projects.

Artificial intelligence can be an important contributor to the innovative process. AI will complement, supplement and verify the human's decisions and choices. The inventor must tune into and listen to the entire mind's ecosystem when making a decision. The most important element in the innovative process is one's passionate and communicated commitment.

7
SEXUALITY, YIN AND YANG

"When we understand and connect with our varying frequencies of Yin and Yang energy, we are able to intimately engage with our partner and enhance our sexuality. Our relationship, when in harmony with our lover, mirrors their proportion of male and female energy and duplicates the requirement for balance in the relationship as a whole.

Karren Whiteley-Brooks, 2010 Thoughts on Energy

While the definition of sexuality is both the "capacity for sexual feelings" and "one's sexual orientation or preference" (*Oxford Dictionary*), I would rather speak about the energy. On some biological and genetic levels, we are programmed with instincts for procreation. These instincts produce a sexual energy which can contribute to our spiritual currency and may be the single most important factor in adding to or detracting from our life's capital. I believe one's orientation toward sexuality is a complex and intricate web of influences which may lose significance and beauty with the mere act of analysis. While science may seem anti-romantic, understanding our personal truth is always beautiful. For me sexuality is a frequency, constantly changing and evolving, and the more we can understand our personal frequency the more we can enjoy our sexuality. I readily admit that I enjoy sex and I enjoy people who enjoy sex; in my experience they are happier, healthier and wealthier, especially in terms of life's capital.

Anthropologists and Sociologists have studied sexual norms and their manifestations in rituals and theologies. In almost every language which has both masculine and feminine delineation, the powerful forces of Sky Father, Heaven, Lightning, Thunder, Sun, Fire and Wind are given masculine gender characteristics, while predominantly most cultures speak of Mother Earth or Earth Mother.

In the Spanish translation, for example, it is: El *Padre Cielo*, El *Cielo*, El *Trueno*, El *Relámpago*, El *Sol*, El *Fuego* y El *Viento contra* La *Madre Tierra o* La *Tierra*. The El is masculine and the La article denotes the feminine adjective in Spanish. Most languages and cultures are similar in this sexual orientation regarding the elements of our existence which permeates our beliefs and, indeed, our very sexuality.

John Maxwell Taylor, in his book *Eros Ascending*, wrote, "When we practice sacred sexuality we are working with cosmologically rooted principles, balancing the heavenly *yang* (male energy) of the universe with the all-knowing, life-giving *yin* (feminine energy) of the earth within ourselves."

There is no doubt that theology and religion have shaped the sexual practices and prejudices over time. Despite a more enlightened and secular society today, the Puritanical and Victorian-inspired ideas continue to influence Western society's sexual norms. Some examination of these historic precepts may help us realise our own sexual orientation, preference and prejudice. Many ancient religions had their own dogma and ritual concerning the sexes and sexuality, and these ideas have relevance for us as we struggle to find our own happiness with our personal sexuality.

The Ancient Romans worshipped Jupiter, who was similar to the Ancient Greek god Zeus. These masculine figures ruled over the more feminine aspects attributed to Earth. Another example is found in the Maori mythology of the Pacific, where Ranginui was the sky father. The myth has Ranginui hug the earth mother, Papatuanuku, and produce divine children. The *Yin* female energy is almost always internalised and depicted in nurturing, fecund, welcoming and receiving descriptions, while the *Yang* male energy is, like the male organ, external, seeking, penetrating, conquering and fertilising. These dualities and differences are not the humorously described emotional orientations of men and women in John Gray's *Venus and Mars*, but the cosmic harmonies of opposites. Light and Dark as well as Life and Death among other dualities are found in each of us in constantly changing amounts. Within our own sexuality, as parts of our whole being, are the more fascinating tidal flows of sexual energies. Earthly manifestations of these powerful forces became objects of worship in ancient cultures as studied by modern anthropologists.

In Wiltshire, England, home to the World Heritage Site of Stonehenge, the frequency of legitimate crop circles caused by meteorological conditions, such as "waterspouts" or mini tornadoes, has been theorised as the inspiration for the original worshipful circles. The Neolithic farmers, it is proposed, saw the brutish *Yang* force of the heavens, which sent lightning bolts and tornadoes to form circular patterns in the crops and penetrate the earth mother, which was worshipped for her *Yin* fertility and abundance. The evidence of burial circles and stones to immortalise the round symbol, usually attributed to the feminine, is a common explanation offered by anthropological specialists. The theories speculate that the use of circles constructed from stone, earth and wood in ancient worship, commemorated the earth mother in a variety of agrarian cultures, which were dependent on the basic weather for their very existence. These cultures witnessed storms which appeared aggressive and developed into a reverence for masculine heavenly powers which took a more piercing and phallic manifestation. The energies of *yin* and *yang* required to fertilise and produce crops and livestock and, indeed, children are the basis for cultural and theological rituals which continue into modern traditions and religions.

The four basic elements of Fire, Wind, Water and Earth are revered and many times given anthropomorphic embodiments.

It is typical that Water and Earth are female figures and Fire and Wind more usually associated with male representatives. The nurturing and *Yin* power of water is eloquently explored by the Japanese author Dr Masaru Emoto in his book *Messages in Water*. While Emoto is frequently criticised for inadequate scientific methodology, it is not difficult to understand how connectivity and positive energy can influence this basic element and in turn how our physical and spiritual health can be affected by the water we consume and contact. Many religions give a blessing with or imbue a spiritual significance to water. The well-known Roman Catholic shrines of Lourdes and Fatima and other centres for healing are dedicated to the Blessed Mary and her feminine grace. The "Holy Water" used in baptisms and in the fonts of most churches is blessed by the priests for the increase of spiritual health of the faithful.

A few years ago, while living in the Middle East, one of our Muslim friends made a pilgrimage to Mecca in Saudi Arabia and brought us back a souvenir. We learned that there is not only the famous Hajj, which is mandated as a requirement for devout Muslims to pursue at least once in their life, but, less well known to Westerners, many devout Islamists make other frequent visits to Mecca, called Umrah. These Umrah visits commemorate the Old Testament Prophet Abraham's second wife (again female involvement), and her search for water to satisfy her thirsty infant son.

The heat and arid climate of Saudi Arabia is well known and, according to Islamic tradition, Hagar walked seven times between the hills of Mecca around 2000 BC. Her maternal sacrifice and inspired intention produced a miraculous discovery of water in the arid valley now called the Valley of Abraham. While we were expecting some delicious Saudi dates from our friends, we were surprised to find our souvenir was a bottle of Zamzam water taken from this Oasis only 20 metres from the sacred Kabaa or cube which Muslims circumnavigate during their Hajj. This Zamzam water is supposedly blessed and again linked to the feminine mother figure of Hagar. The connectivity with motherhood and nurturing and procreation are all important components of our individual sexuality.

The universal traditions surrounding the elements of Water and Earth as feminine elements, continue to be important in modern culture throughout the world. This *Yin* energy is fundamental to the enjoyment and desire of our sexuality, independent of our gender and sexual orientation. The healing aspects of Earth, e.g. mud baths, mineral springs, etc., and Water, including shrines and Holy Water, relate to the healing aspects of sexuality.

When discussing sexual healing, I am not just talking about the emotion expressed in the song of the same name, famously performed by Marvin Gaye, although I do enjoy the music. Actual sexual healing comes from the emotional connection and positive biochemical processes from healthy sexuality.

There are innumerable studies and literature regarding sexual health. Unfortunately, in my opinion, a preponderance of discussion, focus and indeed education surrounds the problems of sexually transmitted diseases and unwanted pregnancies. While these areas of sexual health are important, little focus on the benefits of a healthy sex life and indeed a definition of what good sexual health consists of is avoided in most of the literature. While most Western adolescents are well versed in STDs, very few of them are aware of another type of VD which I like to call "Veering Disease" or the unfortunate behaviour of looking for a different partner and not being present enough to love the one *you are* with; veering from the intense energy required in love.

My research assistant has given me several articles found on the internet site WebMD, which may prove instructive. This chapter is not intended to be a comprehensive examination of sexuality and sexual health. If you have problems which may require medical examination and treatment, then your family physician and this web site may provide guidance.

WebMD did include a list of "10 Surprising Health

Benefits of Sex" (www.webmd.com/sex-relationships/guide/sex-and-health) I leave you to enjoy their compilation, but I was especially impressed that one's immune system benefited from frequent sex. The importance of one's immune system has become an almost daily news item, considering its importance in fighting the Covid-19 virus and indeed, all infections.

At the risk of sounding like a parent encouraging green vegetable consumption, the scientific evidence is overwhelming: sex is good for you.

In Chinese philosophy we can find that like the above symbol, *yin* and *yang* are two parts of the whole. While complementary, they may not always be equally in balance as depicted in the symbol. Whether male or female, we each have, to a greater or lesser extent, elements of the opposite sex. The ability to complement and increase our own *Yin* or *Yang* energy in response to our partner's energy flow increases our romantic ability to invoke heightened sexuality and sexual pleasure for our self and the object of our affections.

While the 20th century saw many of the "glass ceilings" cracked in both the corporate and political worlds, the basic fear of loss of power and *Yang* energy is for me one of the main reasons men refuse to fully "shatter" those sexually discriminating "ceilings". My own experience interacting with powerful men in business is illustrative of what happens every day when men and women come together in the workplace. I was invited to advise and counsel a Fortune 500 company's board of directors, comprised of 15 men and 2 women. One of the women was the Corporate Secretary and, by coincidence, personal secretary to the Chairman Emeritus. The other woman was an elderly and intelligent educator, who was quite vocal about the lack of *Yin* energy on the Board and throughout the company.

After successfully working through a variety of communication problems between the members it was suggested by a couple of directors that they should consider me for a full-time position on the board. My intuition and powers of observation sensed that most of the board was adamantly fearful of the appointment. Never one to shy away from the flow of energy, I stated, after apologising to the two female directors, "Gentlemen, you fear me in the boardroom because you don't know how to manage your erections." They squirmed and understood that I was not speaking about corporate buildings but the normal sexual attraction that younger women can inspire in older *Yang-*

charged magnates of business. On some subconscious spiritual and energetic levels, men know that women can distract, at best, and usurp, at worst, their supposedly required *Yang* energy.

The issue for men and women is understanding and harnessing their sexual energy. The power of position, whether in business or politics, is littered with the refuse of destroyed credibility, because these energies were not controlled. Notably, the Profumo scandal in Britain and the Clinton-Lewinsky scandal in the US are famous for the *Yang* energy run amok. The proliferation of sexual discrimination suits brought by young women, who allege powerful men abuse their position, has led to corporate human resource departments teaching courses in self-control and political correctness as a matter of best practice. The #MeToo movement, which has emboldened women and some men to bring legal cases against powerful men who abused their position, has led to the destruction of careers, including those of comedian Bill Cosby and movie mogul Harvey Weinstein, who has been found guilty of sexual assault. The surprising lack of sexual control and abuse of power is what is common in all of these horrendous incidents.

This requirement for sexual control has been the subject of fables and literature throughout human history. One of my long-time friends, Derek, and senior member of my "Wise Owls Network", who recently passed on, told a traditional story from his native South Africa. He related that Shaka, the famous 19th-century King of the Zulus, used sexual control as a requirement in the training of his young warriors. While many of King Shaka's accomplishments, which include fratricide and slavery trade, are to be reviled, the organisation of his young tribal members and orientation to discipline continues to be revered, especially in military schools. Zulu King Shaka insisted that aspiring warriors must pass all training and abstain from sex until he declared them fit. They were required to run without sandals and become athletically fit and disciplined to control their *yang* energy. It was common practice, relates my South African friend, to march young gorgeous naked virgin girls in front of the aspiring warrior teenage boys. The penalty for any of the undisciplined lads who exhibited attraction which resulted in hardening of their sexual organs was to be immediately put to death. Young women who became pregnant outside of tribally sanctioned marriages were also slain by mandate of King Shaka, which no doubt aided in the maintenance of sexual discipline and abstinence. The issue of sexual discipline is key to the development of healthy sexuality and the ability to manage one's energy.

Modern sport abounds with stories of coaches who require from their young male athletes sexual abstinence before competition. World-class stars such as Muhammad Ali relate the intelligence of a period of abstaining from sex before entering the arena of competition. This is especially popular in those sports which logically require an emotionally *yang*-filled spirit such as boxing, football, martial arts, etc.

Less well publicised is the theory that sports which require more accuracy and peace of mind may be performed more expertly after sexual fulfilment and the possible increase in the competitor's *yang* energy. One US study showed increase muscle strength and oxygen use after sexual intercourse.[1]

Debates as to how much and how frequently sexual intercourse should be enjoyed are less important than the logical focus on the energy required in the act itself. Our personal sexual desires and control are the areas we need to understand in order to feel in harmony with our own ethical requirements. It is this understanding and control which can lead to increased spiritual currency.

As with any physical urge, from hunger to horniness, the control and direction of those urges can lead to increased creativity and connectivity with our spiritual self. In most religions, some sexual abstinence is required as dogma. At times this is just premarital abstinence as a hold-over from pre-contraceptive times, but is in some religions used to mark sacrifice and focus during traditionally important festivals. The sad preponderance of paedophilia in the Catholic Church may argue against sexual abstinence to the extent of celibacy, but there is always a need for self-control.

The use of fasting as a dietary control is practiced by many religions as a way of inspiring spirituality. The issue is not the hunger but the channelling of that energy and focus into a spiritual contemplation. The human difficulty with sexual urges is abstinence can be used as a weapon or game in relationships and in some cases to the detriment of one's own emotional problems. Sex can be an escape and is addictive like all endorphin-producing activities, which include drugs, chocolates and exercise among others. The knowledge that

---

1. *Effects of sexual intercourse on maximal aerobic power, oxygen pulse, and double product in male sedentary subjects.* Boone, T., Gilmore, S. Department of Exercise Physiology, College of St. Scholastica, Duluth, MN. The Journal of Sports Medicine and Physical Fitness, 1995 Sep;35(3):214-7.

sex can produce biochemical triggers is important in the understanding of our attractions and emotional control.

Several years ago, I was working at a spiritual retreat in the United States, a place of contemplation and self-examination. One of the participants who looked to me for leadership and direction humorously reminded me of a story which illustrates that feeling of sexual attraction which can be overwhelming and often arises at the most inappropriate of times.

This student, who later became my friend, and, at the risk of sounding like Clinton, "with whom I never had intimate relations", is a happily married, successful businessman. He reminded me of a situation which happens to most people when they are in a professional relationship with highly energetic persons to whom they could be attracted on a sexual basis.

The student came to visit me and retreated to sit at the far end of the living room. He relates that he recalls I had recently lost my mother to cancer and remembers wanting to comfort me. His empathy was also mixed with a strong sexual attraction, and thus he decided to occupy the chair furthest from me to control his desire. As one does, I moved towards his end of the room, drawn to the unusual vacuum of space between us. While my friend was hoping to increase his ability to control his ill-timed sexual urges by distancing himself, the opposite result occurred as I walked towards him. We laugh now as he says he sincerely feared that I was going to touch him, and he would have been unable to control his urge to embrace me. The confusion of energies, including admiration, empathy and indeed sexuality, can become a jumble that is both exciting and perplexing.

I can recall now and have always had the ability to tune in to other people's energy and intentions. Sexual attraction is normal and can be flattering when both parties keep their urges in check and directed on a respectful and appropriate basis. I smile warmly at the memory of that visit despite the energetic and emotional turmoil.

Flirting is the common manifestation of sexual attraction. The question becomes: do you know when you are flirting and when someone is flirting with you? Being in tune with, and sensitive to, the sexual connectivity which is common in all humans is important to understand and control the energy flow of sexuality and increase our spiritual currency.

The power and charisma of the most successful humans is often accompanied by an ability to be attractive on a sexual level. Those most successful and most spiritual humans can harness and channel their sexual energy and transmute that power into productive and creative activities. If one analyses the most productive outcomes of sexuality, the inescapable conclusion is that three main results are most desirable:

1st – Procreation, which is the DNA programme for the propagation of the species.

2nd – The expression of love, which both spiritually and physically, contributes to better health. Evidence is overwhelming that people in love and sexually fulfilled are mentally and spiritually healthier than those without a partner.

3rd – The transference of romantic energy, the transmutation of sexuality into a productive endeavour, e.g. business, art, spirituality and all desirable pursuits.

While the obvious and simple reason that humans can enjoy their sexuality is procreation, what is more complicated is the human ability to control and transmute that energy for other purposes.

If we can agree that sexual desire increases our awareness and connectivity with our fellow man, then it is worth examining the biochemical evidence of our hormonal urges.

If educators truly understood the profound implications for young women and men's sexuality as it relates to the monthly hormonal cycle, sex education would be far more important and comprehensive. It appears to me that, in most Western societies, what is euphemistically called "sex education" is long on biology and almost devoid of spirituality and ethics as it relates to this most important of life's energy. What happens in the hormonal cycle in a woman's menstrual and ovulation periods is more complex and complicated than the well reported pre-menstrual syndrome (PMS), which has been reduced to the butt of sitcom jokes and entirely misunderstood.

I would examine the female cycle as it relates to the emotional response which is triggered by the hormonal variation. Less scientific and more energetic examination is necessary to understand and relate the cyclical variation which both men and women feel. For me and many of my female acquaintances, a nesting and home-oriented feeling is normal before our menstruation. Partners should be aware of these feelings and reduce their aggressively charged approaches by providing more *yin*-oriented encounters in order to complement their partner's hormonal change.

I have been complimented by many women friends after discussing my simple, non-scientific, explanation for the sadness that is often produced during menstruation. I believe if our animal DNA has programmed our biochemistry to produce the urge to procreate, it is logical that on various levels a woman is disappointed when she begins her monthly period. When a woman finds she is not pregnant, as evidenced by her menstrual flow, which expels her unused egg and preparatory nutrients, it is a symbolic failure. The menstruating woman's feelings of loss and melancholy can turn to anger and possibly depression. A US friend told me that in her youth it was common to vulgarly call this withdrawn, sad and sometimes aggressive menstrual state as "OTR" or "on the rag". I like to accentuate the healthiness of the cleansing aspect of menstruation. On some biochemical level our primary procreative function has failed and, like any of our realisations, we must allow our awareness to improve our emotional response to the hormonal influences.

Another important recognition which women are not usually taught in their sex education is that the menstrual cycle is the maximum detox and the opportunity to freshen the uterus and rid the female body of the unused and deteriorating placenta components. A feeling of lightness and cleanliness is a normal emotional response to the end of menstruation. What is less recognised is what the female body and accompanying hormones are preparing for in around two weeks' time.

Ovulation in most women produces some discomfort and definite changes in demeanour. It is normal and logical for most women to be more highly aggressive and sexual towards prospective partners during their ovulation. Some men have told me they can sense and indeed smell when a woman is ovulating. If you have been around a stud farm then you will have witnessed a stallion who is definitely aroused by the smell of a willing mare in heat. The distortion of the stallion's nostrils as he smells the pheromone-charged secretions of the mare produces a sexual excitement that not even the discipline of King Shaka could control.

I call my ovulation, with apologies to truck drivers, my "even a lorry driver will do" time of the month. I mean that my hormones and urge to procreate make my drive to copulate difficult to control. A variety of studies have shown that our ability to find fertile and chemically compatible partners is assisted by our secreted pheromones and our sub-conscious response to fulfilling our 'propagation' programme. The act of kissing is not just foreplay, but a chemical examination of our partner's saliva which can stimulate or repel our attraction. Several studies have confirmed that we use our senses of smell and taste to find a partner with different immune-system chemistry in order to improve the chance of survival for our offspring and indeed, the species. While the scent of romantic flowers, perfumes and colognes have become multi-billion-dollar business, biochemistry promises to become increasingly important in the Valentine Days of the future.

A fascinating study showed that waitresses earned bigger tips by a factor of almost three during their time of ovulation, and that gratuities were smaller during the time of their menstruation. The scientists believe that demeanour as well as the pheromone odours were both contributing factors in this anomaly.

At the University of North Carolina, J. Richard Udry studied the relationship between coitus, orgasm and timing within the menstrual cycle. The study determined that women engage in sexual intercourse about six times more frequently around the time of ovulation, when women's sensitivity to the male pheromonal odour is most acute. More interesting is the link between smell and sexuality, which found women are more likely to have an orgasm during ovulation. Women in Udry's study were less likely to have either sexual intercourse or an orgasm by a significant factor in the first few days following menstruation. A direct relationship between women's sensitivity to the musky smell of men, which can be related to the female period, is seldom discussed in sex education classes. Maybe teachers should be giving out nose-plugs with their free condoms?

Men are also responding to the smell of ovulating women's pheromones more than perfume and they feel more sexually charged. When male hormones are stimulated by pheromones and the women's fervent intention, the most disciplined celibate has a greatly reduced chance to resist. The effects of the hormonal attractions and the sexual advances of prospective partners can be emotionally charged. Despite our rational brain protesting and attempting to avoid a sexual encounter without the requisite romance and ticking of our ideal-partner boxes, our animal instincts may win out.

Sexual frustration is the blocking of energy and life force and can be transmuted by those who understand the biological and emotional influences and rechannelling of these forces. Those who can convert this energy into creative activities include those historic achievers who find a positive outlet for their energy.

The symbolic act of fertilisation in all animals, but especially humans, is depicted in a variety of pictograms and icons, but for me the best representation is the Mobius Loop, symbolic of our Spiritual currency. The mathematical complexity of this symbol is the fact that it traces a total connection and has no beginning or end. While there are obviously two loops they are in harmony and flowing one into another without end. Love, which culminates in a sexual act can feel like that, with the energy flowing and circulating and not limited to terminating boundaries.

Human sexuality is ideally fulfilled with orgasm, not just as an act of passion or lust, but, unlike other animals, includes the expression of love. An interesting debate is whether one can have heightened sexuality without love. One can certainly have sex without love. It is thought that the animalistic and biological imperative to procreate, with accompanying passion, pleasure and orgasmic contractions which humans feel, is similarly experienced in other animals. Love and the emotional and intellectual aspects of sexuality are only found in the human species.

If love is the most powerful of energies and sexuality is an outcome of our evolutionary program to procreate, then the most fulfilling and energising use of one's sexuality is as an expression of love. Powerful beings, whom we may encounter in business and other life situations, are typically sexually attractive, even if their age, body types and aesthetic appeal are not ideal. Most probably, you have met people who inspired an emotional conflict and possibly guilty feeling, because on some level we felt an inappropriate sexual attraction. I laugh that my encounter with His Holiness, the Dalai Lama, inspired in me a visceral desire to have "Dalai babies".

In several languages and cultures, the sexual orgasm is compared to death, e.g. in the French expression *la petite mort*. The ecstasy both men and women feel after orgasm, begs the question "Is this frequent description, the freedom of death which we glimpse in orgasm or the glimpse of death we feel in the release experienced from the orgasm?"

Less poetic than *la petite mort* is the scientific explanation that, after orgasm, the brain releases the chemical *oxytocin* in both men and women. So, while there are huge physical differences between the orgasmic contractions, and their frequency and intensity, for men and women the neurochemicals produced in orgasm result in similar experiences for both sexes in similar proportions. Recent studies have shown that *oxytocin*, which is a neuromodulating hormone produced in the pituitary glands of both men and women, has an important role in bonding of couples and parents to their children. As an example, *oxytocin* is produced when breastfeeding infants, and one of the reasons the brain can confuse this maternal act with sexual stimulation.

While the complexity of the emotional and physical aspects of sexuality will continue to be studied and romanticised in literature and advertising, the magnitude of the energy generated through our sexuality will always be the most important factor in enriching our life's capital. If we can embrace our sexuality and search for a partner of similar energy and romantic goals, then the love generated will be the motor propelling our spirituality.

Love is the most powerful force which exists in our universe. Love is without absence, so the more present we can be, the more love we can feel. Love is a natural phenomenon and occurs with the presence we can generate by affection and focus on our partner, complementing the tidal changes in their *yin* and *yang* balance to enhance our own personal frequency. It is through love that our sexuality is fully realised.

> *"Once the realisation is accepted that even between the closest human beings infinite distances continue, a wonderful living side by side can grow, if they succeed in loving the distance between them which makes it possible for each to see the other whole against the sky."*
> *Rainer Maria Rilke*

8.
LOVE, OMNIPRESENCE, AND SOVEREIGNTY

"L.O.V.E." Lustrous, Omnipresent, Virtuous, Energy
Karren Whiteley-Brooks

After a chapter on sexuality, to follow with thoughts about L.O.V.E. seems as out of order as the proverbial "cart before the horse". My mother, who continues to speak with me from another dimension, and her generation would counsel that love and, indeed, marriage, or at the very least commitment, should be present before any contemplation of sexual intimacy. Anything else was not what good girls would do. But, like most commandments, the realities of the ethical conundrums are more complex.

For me L.O.V.E. can be better understood as an acronym: *lustrous, omnipresent, virtuous, energy*. Love is *lustrous*, that shining, shimmering and glittering quality; what the younger generation would describe as the ultimate "bling". To be in love and to give and receive love, one must be present, but for me the best love and, indeed, the best lovers are *omnipresent*, and that is to be connected to everything and everywhere concerned with their universe. By definition love is *virtuous*, because it embodies all that is good. And last in my acronym for love is the "e" for *energy*. Anything which can move and change and influence our lives and those of others as much as love must be an *energy*. The energy of love is no less powerful than the attraction of gravity and no less changeable than the direction of the wind. Love may be similarly invisible, as those physical energies, but no less real.

In this Chapter we will discuss more about connectivity with our past, present and future existence. You may have great scepticism and would be in good company, if you doubt that there is an afterlife or, even more difficult to comprehend, previous lives. I won't try to convince you one way or another, but I will state unequivocally that connectivity is of prime importance in the growth of your Spiritual Currency and Life's Capital.

We jealously hold on to belief systems which are comfortable and maintain our ignorance. When we contemplate the energy of love and the connectivity and responsibility inherent in participating in that energy, we expand our spirituality. The thought of each of us in our insignificance on this "pale blue dot" makes us grow through the connectivity with each of our kindred spirits who inhabit our current, past and indeed future universe.

We began this chapter speaking about L.O.V.E. and how the energy is virtuous. It requires the permeation of the spiritual energy of our lover to feel the virtue and experience the lustre of the connection. This is not merely the giddy and passionate enjoyment of a lustful physical intimacy, which can be an expression of love and can also be experienced without love. The emotional and physical contact between humans expressed in lust may be as spiritual and fulfilling or as momentary and ephemeral as the intention and attention allows. It depends on each of us if we chose to, with our firm intention, experience the depth and beauty of permeating the object of our love and embracing their spirit, not just their body. All too often our human and biological attractions take precedence over our virtuous intention to connect with and permeate the spirit of our lover.

If I could discuss with my mother her admonition of love before intimacy, I would expand her suggestion to require spiritual permeation and the intention to experience my partner with an omnipresence, which requires a greater commitment. Maybe I have come to these conclusions, inspired by my dialogue with her on another plane and by connecting with her spirit, unencumbered by the limitations of her human body and motherly role.

When we think about love, we almost always contemplate a rather small circle of family and relatives. If we answer that famous song's question "Who do you love?" the human response is usually our romantic partner, our immediate family or the occasional media idol in the entertainment or sport's world. Most of us treat love as if it were a limited resource, to be meted out sparingly, to fewer rather than more people. Some years ago, I was living in Dubai and went on a trip across the desert. In preparation we took a great deal of water despite driving a new and reliable vehicle… just in case. Having lived my life in countries where potable water was always plentiful, the precaution to take water on our journey was a new experience. Possibly the human orientation to love is confused with the evolutionary imperative to have enough water and other resources required for survival.

For all too many of us love is not easy to give or to receive. Seldom in my experience, when one is described as being exceedingly loving, is that description considered positive. All too often, for those few individuals who are described as "too loving", we usually add descriptions of being too trusting, or being naive. It is as if love requires innocence, and, like our skin, wrinkles and withers with experience and age. Love produces energy, not saps energy. Love engenders spirituality and in an unending Mobius loop, increases and continues regenerating itself. Love is a limitless resource.

When I look at the acronym L.O.V.E., I recall how difficult it has been to describe the beauty of the emotional experience and baffled poets and philosophers over the ages. When we release our ego and surrender to our spirituality, we can attain the omnipresence required to be a good lover. It is, of course, the excitement and thrill of the physical connection which commands volumes of advice and explanation. True love, which requires sovereignty, is on a much higher plane and supersedes any of the normal relationship games of possession and submission. This greater love eliminates the perspective of yours and mine and becomes truly "'ours".'

When that virtuous wave of energy comes from the depths of our hearts, it is transformative and healing. Pure love does not care about differences; it only functions on the level which unites us as one humanity. To open our hearts to the connection with everything, allows us to experience the infinite possibilities of love.

The good news is, as we invest in our Spiritual Currency, we receive the dividend of omnipresence which allows us to experience, L.O.V.E. Like any productive account, our Life's Capital grows through the magic of love's compounding energy.

We all would like to have more love in our life and by recognizing the universality of that emotion and acting on it, like magic it happens. We can give more love and in turn automatically receive more love in the Karmic miracle of multiplicity which is this: L.ustrous O.mnipresent V.irtuous E.nergy.

> *"All you need is love."*
> *John Lennon*

You may have lost a loved one in your immediate family, as I did with my mother, who died way too young but continues to influence my existence. Take a moment to think about this person, and how they contributed to your ideas and your current life. When we remember our deceased "loved ones", we remain connected. Many would argue that those are just fond memories or, if you feel the dearly departed speaking from beyond, it is often explained as the mind's tricks of reassembling past experiences to appear as if they were new communications.

Please turn to CONTEMPLATION 8. on PASSION Book of Y.O.U.

While psychological explanations have merit, the electron microscope allows us to witness in the sub-particle universe, incontrovertible evidence of current events being influenced by the past. More remarkable and counterintuitive are the molecular movements which can be changed by the mere act of observation; changing and shaping the future. Quantum physics offers additional scientific explanation of the irrelevance of our normal understanding of time. Indeed, humanity's limited knowledge of our universe is just beginning to forward scientific theories for aspects of our life, which were previously debated by philosophers and theologians, never by physicists.

When we think of our treasured memories, it is normal to adjust our mental images to accommodate and improve the reality. Time and other dimensions, when experienced in later life, are remarkably distorted. You may have returned to a place you remember from childhood after being away for many years, and the house or the tree or the hill, which your mind has categorised as huge, now appear smaller and inconsequential. You may also remember past relationships which ended with disappointments and find it difficult to conjure anything but positives from the experience. Yes, our mind plays tricks, but the more we contemplate our past and future and our connectivity to all dimensions of time and space, the more spiritual will be our current understanding.

The title of this Chapter, 'Omnipresence, Sovereignty and Love', may sound like a wide range of themes and concepts but, as we seek to grow our Life's Capital, the links may prove instructive. When we contemplate omnipresence, it is almost always used as a description reserved for God or the gods from ancient philosophy. In almost every theology the ability to be omnipresent is reserved for the divine and it should be.

To connect with everything, and to be everywhere, may

appear to be impossible, but it's not. The divine and spiritual aspect in each of us is truly the manifestation of God within and, by definition, links us to our entire universe. It is our humanity, with our physical limitations, which get in the way of our spirituality. The author of the magical Narnia books, C.S. Lewis, said, "You don't have a soul, you are a soul… you have a body." We are, on a spiritual level, automatically connected and like gravity, we are energetically attracted to each other and pulled to the collective spirituality. For many of us spirituality is also like gravity, insofar as it's invisible and difficult to understand.

Try this simple process which was taught to me and I have shared with many others seeking a clearer view of the existence of spirituality. First, may I ask *you*, "Do *you* have a body?" (*You* of course answered, "YES.") Now, may I ask *you*, "Do *you* have a mind?" (*You* of course, again answered, "YES.") Now we ask and contemplate, "Who is the *YOU* who has these things?"

We seldom think about gravity, unless we are watching a space exploration movie, but as Carl Sagan says, "Without gravitational energy all life would cease to exist because our oxygen-enriched atmosphere would float off into space." Without our Life's Capital, which is enriched as we contemplate our spirituality, we would be doomed to the despair of those who believe that this world and this body and this life is all that there is: a lucky cosmic coincidence.

If love is *omnipresent*, as I would argue, then what does that really mean? Often found in the descriptions of omnipresence is the word "ubiquitous", or being everywhere. The golden arches of McDonald's and the red-and-white design of Coca-Cola may be brands which are described as ubiquitous, but not in North Korea. The idea of omnipresence is the ability to connect with everything in our universe. It is much easier than finding a fast-food meal in Pyongyang.

The connections required for omnipresence can only happen when we can command our sovereignty. The idea of being sovereign is not like England's claim to the Falklands or Ukraine's claim on the Crimea. No, when we contemplate the sovereign, it is not to be a monarch or politically powerful, but to be expert in, and in charge of our existence. Take a moment to realize, in what aspect of life are you *expert*? You may have heard of the 10,000 hours required for true expertise proposed by Malcolm Gladwell in his book *Outliers* and debated by many others, who believe practice is more important than talent.

www.bbc.co.uk/news/magazine-26384712

I mention the idea of expertise because many people do not believe they are expert in anything, much less spirituality. For most adults who have a skill, a profession or only a passionate avocation, they are experts. Our rejection of ego usually dictates that someone else labels us an expert or some educational institution bestows a title or license, conferring letters, e.g. MD, PhD, CPA, etc., to indicate our area of sovereignty. It is this rejection of the confidence required to accept our sovereign dominion of personal spirituality, which may interfere with our ability to connect and indeed to love. You may not have dedicated 10,000 hours to practice a certain skill but most of us have contemplated spirituality and our existence for much more time than many believe is required for expertise.

I often help clients understand that they are already spiritual and that they don't need to be in a religious retreat in order to become sovereign over their existence. When we think of someone who is a spiritually wealthy person, we often think of an iconic individual like the aforementioned Dalai Lama or someone removed from our normal world. The techniques of meditation, introspection and contemplation may assist in our quest for spiritual sovereignty but, like most expertise, spirituality is a chosen passion. If we take ten thousand hours of our life as the average amount of required dedication and focus to become expert, then even if you have no title; you have easily contemplated your existence, your purpose and your role in the universe for enough time to make you sovereign. That spiritual contemplation produces the energy required in love and connectivity with our fellow man. The reality is that most humans prefer to ignore this connectivity; we often chose to remain unaware.

"Ignorance is bliss" is a popular saying which I would paraphrase as "choosing not to know what we know". To ignore our connectivity alleviates the responsibility we each have: to care for our universe, which includes our planet and every fellow human. If one is to grow in spirituality, the acceptance of our intuition and knowledge of the energetic connections which exist for all of us, is the first step toward the sovereignty which can evolve to omnipresence.

It is easy to avoid or ignore the universe; it seems so vast and difficult to comprehend. While most of us find the complexity of the universe difficult, one way to understand our planet and our existence is by listening to the author and cosmologist, Carl Sagan. In his book, *Pale Blue Dot*, this astrophysicist explains in layman's terms what the universe and our small planet mean in terms of position and relevance. The inspiration for Sagan's book came from a photo taken by the Voyager Space Probe from a distance of over 3.5 billion miles from Earth. Carl Sagan summarises our position: "In all this vastness there is no hint that help will come from elsewhere to save us from ourselves."

www.youtube.com/watch?v=wupToqz1e2g

While the author argues that we have a responsibility to our *Pale Blue Dot*, you may waver between a feeling of insignificance and a fear that, maybe, we are truly alone. While a humbling treatise, when we consider the cosmos explained by an expert, I think the more important point is our connectivity to all this universe, each other and all that has come before and will exist after our current life.

Most of us reject our personal sovereignty and are afraid of our true power and spirituality. In many theologies the creation of man is as an extension of, or in the image of, the Divine Creator. Whether you believe in God or a Supreme Creator is less important for this introspection than the recognition of each human's spirituality. Just as financial billionaires don't necessarily require a doctorate in economics to be wealthy, riches in spiritual terms simply requires a recognition of our mystical energy and connectivity with our universe, not a Doctorate in Divinity. It is this connectivity which can lead to the sovereignty over our existence and the ability to love.

I have met highly spiritual people who were passionate deists and some could be classified as fervently religious. I have also met very spiritual people who were adamantly agnostic or at least atheistic, so I offer no conclusion as to which school of thought is to be preferred. The following argument is an interesting viewpoint and may require rereading to fully absorb the thought process:

"*Supposing there was no intelligence behind the universe, no creative mind. In that case, nobody designed my brain for the purpose of thinking. It is merely that when the atoms inside my skull happen, for physical or chemical reasons, to arrange themselves in a certain way, this gives me, as a by-product, the sensation I call thought. But, if so, how can I trust my own thinking to be true? It's like upsetting a milk jug and hoping that the way it splashes itself will give you a map of London. But if I can't trust my own thinking, of course I can't trust the arguments leading to Atheism, and therefore have no reason to be an Atheist, or anything else. Unless I believe in God, I cannot believe in thought: so, I can never use thought to disbelieve in God.*"

C. S. Lewis

When we explore the energy of connectivity, we must explore the exchange of one entity with another. It can be the exchange between two beings or the exchange we each experience with events in our lives, including not only past and present, but since we can envision an outcome, I would argue, we can exchange with our future. When people ask me what omnipresence feels like, I remember the description by a client and friend who had that moment of clarity which permeated his existence and led him to describe what is, by definition, intangible in understandable, physical terms. He said to me, "It feels wonderful," and went on to describe the feeling "as if my blood was warmed in my veins and the energy and flow from and through my heart was easier and more pleasant". The spiritual aspect of our being has a demonstrable physical effect on our bodies. Those people who concentrate on their connectivity are happier and healthier.

At the risk of sounding pedantic and old-fashioned, we all remember the maxim: "It is better to give than to receive." That was usually told to us as children, around the holidays, when we had to spend our money on presents for relatives we barely knew. I have come to believe it is better to exchange. Those who are spiritually wealthy learn how to both receive and give appreciations.

You may remember the American indigenous elder who likened his good and bad side to two dogs. The DOG FOOD exercise is an inventory to help you understand and control what you are feeding those dogs.

CONTEMPLATION 9: Book of Y.O.U. DOG FOOD

One of my teachers described this spiritual exchange as a "transceiver", that is to say an instrument, which can both transmit and receive. This image reminds me of my three brothers and me, when we were given toy walkie-talkie sets one Christmas. The four battery operated handsets were classical "transceivers" which could both broadcast and amplify the other callers' voices. Like all games and indeed, communication, certain modalities and rules had to be established with our walkie talkies. We decided that we each had to say "over" when we finished talking and that we would have to take turns playing James Bond. We were all excited to be British spies, and this was the time of Sean Connery, Roger Moore, Britt Eckland and Ursula Andress playing the dashing characters in the 007 universe.

If we didn't follow the rules of the game no one could hear or broadcast, and communication was blocked. All too often communication and exchange of information is similarly focused on what we are saying, rather than listening and exchanging. Like handsets with the broadcast keys pressed simultaneously, a worthwhile exchange is impossible.

Good transceivers are good listeners and seldom judgemental. They help us articulate our feelings and connect with our intentions, which make us feel comfortable and appreciative to have a duplication of our message. The most connected people are excellent transceivers, who know how to listen and speak with wisdom and experience which enhances our communication.

The idea of exchange or a trade between transceivers is one of the distinguishing features of higher life forms. The idea of specialisation for human activity is theorised to have begun over 100,000 years ago when hunters would exchange their protein kill for gatherers' collections of nuts and berries. Later agriculture would evolve and increased specialisation and the corresponding economic exchange fuelled further development of society and cultures. Later still, a substitute currency was recognised to facilitate this economic exchange. Depending on the culture, it may have been beads, or pearls, or bits of gold or silver which became coins later, but the principle of a symbolic store of value is key in economic development.

The symbolic measure of our omnipresence is another way to describe love. If we truly love ourselves and our universe and, indeed, our fellow man, then we can measure our spiritual wealth in millions of *Mobius* energy coins. The wealth of our spiritual currency allows us to exchange and experience the enrichment of true love. Unlike economic currency, our life's capital does not experience inflation or devaluation.

An example would be a current millionaire in Brazil in their local currency, the Real, which has less than half that acquisition value in US dollar terms, despite the currency being launched in 1994 at a parity of one Real to one US dollar. Worse yet, the former currency in Brazil, the cruzeiro, was devalued over 100,000 times in the decades of the 70s and 80s. Spiritual currency maintains its value and, to complete the analogy, holds its exchange buying power to add to our Life's Capital.

When we examine the energy of love, we understand that it allows us to exchange and free ourselves with the stuck forces of self-absorption and egocentrism. As we grow in our spiritual belief and connectivity we grow in rapport with ourselves and our position and responsibility vis-à-vis others. For me the question is not Shakespeare's famous, "to be or not to be", but more importantly, "to know or not to know"; to be aware, that is the real quandary which we must answer to achieve greater spirituality.

9
SLEEP AND PRODUCTIVITY

"Sleep is the rate of interest we have to pay on the capital which is called in at death; and the higher the rate of interest and the more regularly it is paid, the further the date of redemption is postponed."
Arthur Schopenhauer, On the Fourfold Root of the
Principle of Sufficient Reason

Read any book on WELLNESS and the problems of sleep and sleep disorders are usually analysed. Rather than prescribe any habit changes to your life, it may be helpful to consider sleep, as did Schopenhauer, the 19th-century German philosopher. We may paraphrase Schopenhauer to include the concept of Spiritual Currency which is, most certainly, compounded by restful sleep.

First, the question of how much sleep is enough or too much? Thomas Edison said, "People will not only do what they like to do — they overdo it 100 per cent. Most people overeat 100 per cent, and oversleep 100 per cent, because they like it. That extra 100 per cent makes them unhealthy and inefficient. The person who sleeps eight or ten hours a night is never fully asleep and never fully awake – they have only different degrees of doze through the twenty-four hours. For myself I never found need of more than four- or five-hours' sleep in the twenty-four. I never dream. It's real sleep. When by chance I have taken more, I wake dull and indolent. We are always hearing people talk about 'loss of sleep' as a calamity.

They better call it loss of time, vitality and opportunities. Just to satisfy my curiosity I have gone through files of the British Medical Journal and could not find a single case reported of anybody being hurt by loss of sleep. Insomnia is different entirely – but some people think they have insomnia if they can sleep only ten hours every night."

Unless one invents something equally useful, comparable to the light bulb, Edison has doomed each of us to a feeling of inferiority and laziness if we sleep more than "four or five" hours a night. Apparently, Edison did allow himself what are called today "power naps". It has been shown that short 5-30-minute naps can increase productivity and creativity. Many societies permit and encourage an afternoon nap or what the Latinos call "siesta". Most of us can admit to an occasional day of tiredness and usually following a restless night of inadequate sleep, and so the concept of quality of sleep is contemplated.

When researching the area of sleep, it is always useful to consult the experts. One important study was conducted by NASA, who employ sleep researchers, in a quest to understand the optimum amount of sleep for astronauts and suggest best practices. They concluded after exhaustive studies, that eight hours was the optimum amount of sleep for peak performance. After studying hundreds of hours of manned flight statistics they found that despite their recommendations and scheduling of eight hours of sleep, their astronauts were only able to sleep six to six and a half hours on average. A variety of causes from weird noises to weightlessness were cited as the reasons for not being able to attain the recommended eight hours of sleep. NASA then concluded that naps were beneficial and scientifically measured that memory retention, stamina and improved motor skills could all be significantly increased by napping. One study proved that with a nap of 26 minutes increased performance of "working memory", defined as the ability to focus attention on one task while holding other tasks in memory, could be improved by 34 per cent. NASA continues to schedule eight hours of sleep for their manned missions, but now includes a 30-minute nap during the working day.

So how much is enough and how much is too much when it comes to sleep? Most studies conclude that eight hours with an approximate deviation of up to 25%, or two hours, more or less, can be considered sufficient sleep in order to maintain wellness. The personal variation, based on a variety of factors including physical activity and respiratory health, lead to large variations from the suggested norm.

In my non-scientific laboratory of experience with clients looking for increased spiritual currency, the areas of time and sleep are often the two most important themes. It has been my experience that sleeping more than 10 hours per night is a strong indicator of a depressive state for an individual who prefers avoiding rather than confronting the problems of one's existence.

Any increase in Spiritual Currency requires an awareness and dedication to our physical health and one irrefutable necessity is an alert mental capacity produced by quality sleep. David Dinges, a professor at the University of Pennsylvania School of Medicine, conducted a study funded by NASA which demonstrated that vigilance and basic alertness were not increased by napping. You may be well within the daily sleep guidelines of the 25% less or more than eight hours (or between six and ten hours), but still not feel rested? You may also wish to increase your alertness and ability to confront life's issues? You may have concluded that if I sleep just one hour less, I can increase my productivity by 5 to 10%. Unfortunately, the reverse result is the more common outcome if we deprive ourselves of sleep. You may continue to feel guilty if you sleep eight hours, and the American author Tom Wolfe humorously reversed this fear of lethargy as follows:

"Then people say you're a glutton for work, but it isn't so. It's laziness – just plain, damned, simple laziness, that's all...

Napoleon – and Balzac – and Thomas Edison – these fellows who never sleep more than an hour or two at a time, and can keep going night and day – why that's not because they love to work! It's because they're really lazy – and afraid not to work because they know they're lazy! Why, hell yes!... I'll bet you anything you like if you could really find out what's going on in old Edison's mind, you'd find that he wished he could stay in bed every day until two o'clock in the afternoon! And then get up and scratch himself! And then lie around in the sun for a while! And hang around with the boys down at the village store, talking about politics, and who's going to win the World Series next fall!"

Thomas Wolfe, You Can't Go Home Again

If our quest to increase Spiritual Currency requires wellness, then an alert mind and well-rested body are fundamental to that healthy existence. Interestingly absent is any scientific research by NASA into the increase of mental alertness using meditation. Possibly governmental agencies fear criticism for spending taxpayer money in areas that may be linked with spirituality? One would assume, incorrectly, that galactic exploration by NASA would require more investigation of the spiritual side of mental functionality. As spirituality becomes more desirable and accepted by society, we can expect more funded research into areas of meditation and contemplation as it relates to brain function.

A study published in the *Harvard Gazette* describes an eight-week programme of mindfulness meditation, which used MRI (Magnetic Resonance Imaging) from the Massachusetts General Hospital and Harvard School of Medicine in order to measure and demonstrate physical changes in the brain after meditation: "Meditation group participants reported spending an average of 27 minutes each day practicing mindfulness exercises, and their responses to a mindfulness questionnaire indicated significant improvements compared with pre-participation responses. The analysis of MR images, which focused on areas where meditation-associated differences were seen in earlier studies, found increased grey-matter density in the hippocampus, known to be important for learning and memory, and in structures associated with self-awareness, compassion, and introspection."

Participant-reported reductions in stress also were correlated with decreased grey-matter density in the *amygdala*, which is known to play an important role in anxiety and stress. Although no change was seen in a self-awareness-associated structure called the *insula*, which had been identified in earlier studies, the authors suggest that longer-term meditation practice might be needed to produce changes in that area: "None of these changes were seen in the control group, indicating that they had not resulted merely from the passage of time."

If we seek more connectivity and awareness through better mental health, then meditation, when combined with adequate sleep and restful naps, can provide an even greater increase than any time gained through sleep deprivation. Meditation promotes presence and self-awareness and knowingness which increases productivity. There are a variety of great books and websites dedicated to meditation, and in future iterations of *Spiritual Currency – Life's Capital* we will publish our readers preferences and anecdotes.

In a recent report by the National Sleep Foundation in their Bedroom Poll, less than half of people in the United States, Canada, United Kingdom, and Germany reported a "good night's sleep", and Japan had only a slightly higher result at 54%. Russel Rosenberg PhD, Director of Research, NSF and Investigator at NeuroTrials Research says, "This ground-breaking poll suggests that chronic sleep deprivation is a significant global health problem... setting the stage for good sleep can change your life."

We are constantly meeting experts in the field of sleep research and would offer the following "Top Ten" suggestions as well as some scientific explanation as to why the conventional wisdom is not always correct. Many of us in the UK are used to a hot bath before bed, considering it to be relaxing. Research has demonstrated that sleep in all animals is more restful and usually occurs at 3–5% less body temperature. The science would argue for a cool wash before bed rather than a hot bath or shower.

Please feel free to send us your best ideas and any expert evidence as to why your suggestions may work. We will update our suggestions and incorporate the latest research and readers' best practices.

The following list is for those of us who would like to sleep better and be more rested; it is not meant for chronic insomniacs or those with physical disabilities such as apnoea. If you are consistently getting less than six hours' sleep in a 24-hour cycle over a period of more than a week, then you should consult a medical professional. Despite what Thomas Edison may have thought, it is now accepted science that humans require at least six hours of sleep on a consistent basis. The following outline of more restful sleep practices is an outlined compilation of the latest research.

PREPARE YOURSELF TO SLEEP

While preparation in anything is always good advice, experts from the National Sleep Foundation have suggested that preparing for bed at least 30 minutes before reclining is very important for a successful rest. They advise that our bedtime preparation includes three important components: (A) lower light, (B) lower temperature and (C) a normal routine. They suggest:

A. TURN OFF all electronics… telephones, tablets, TV's PC's, and Wi-Fi at least 30 minutes before bed. Let our eyes rest, preferably in a minimal amount of light. Our minds and biological clocks are very light-sensitive, and bright lights from screens and often in our bathrooms are counterproductive to our sleep preparation. A completely darkened bedroom, and possibly a sleep blindfold, will help our body know that it is time to rest. For those of us who may use our bed as a place to write, converse and recreate by watching a screen, it is important to cease this activity 30 minutes before reclining. The suggestion to have a bedside pad and pencil for any good idea or night-time epiphany will increase our feeling of tranquillity.

We enjoy connection, and the urge to check our emails just one more time may be overwhelming. You may think, as do many of my clients, that you are more tranquil if you know you are connected in case a relative could need you. Those of us who may wish to ensure that we could be awakened in case of emergency should limit that access to our landline, which only rings from a direct call, without beeping and dinging with every email and text message. Wind down your attention to new thoughts and begin a routine which becomes almost robotic and hypnotic in its repetitive aspects. After due preparation the routine should be with incrementally decreasing light and energy. Humans sleep better in darkness, and once again we can fault Edison for producing artificial light, which disturbs our sleep cycle.

B. LOWER TEMPERATURE
18–22 degrees Celsius is considered optimum temperature for sleeping, so turn the thermostat down. With the increasing cost of heating and energy in general, the added savings will help you sleep more peacefully. A lighter duvet is recommended with the caveat that one should never feel cold or chilled.

C. ROUTINE
Think about what you usually do before bed. Most of us check our doors and windows; possibly putting out or in a pet is part of the routine. Hygiene, which may include a facial and skin moisturizing for most women and some of my male friends, is a great routine. Most people like to brush their teeth, and

gargling a mentholated disinfectant may help our respiration and decrease snoring and apnea.

Having lived in the Middle East and watched the ritual Islamic ablutions, I was instructed that most Arabs wash their feet just before bedtime. This is not just a religious tradition but also a logical step, in that dust particles may accumulate on the soles of our feet and rinsing them helps one sleep.

As one reclines, a review of the day, which includes a mental thank you for all the seen and unseen positive thoughts and occurrences, is a healthy mental routine. The iconic idea of counting sheep as a sure way to fall asleep may indeed work. Watching and numbering the sheep in our mind's eye achieves a meditative state of not allowing our mind to think about the normal worries and concerns.

We have spoken of meditation in a separate chapter, but many people swear by the tranquillity and calming effect which meditation has before bed. While it may be just a song first popularized in the 1954 movie *White Christmas*, then sung by Bing Crosby and more recently Diana Krall, these lyrics may help with your sleep problems and are preferable to sheep.

> *"If you're worried and you can't sleep*
> *Just count your blessings instead of sheep*
> *And you'll fall asleep*
> *Counting your blessings"*
>
> *Irving Berlin, 1954 White Christmas*

Here is a simple inventory of good sleep habits.

SLEEP INVENTORY

The following exercise is an inventory of your environment and habits which may contribute to your feeling of inadequate rest. Before you begin ask yourself on a scale of 1 (poor) to 100 (excellent), how restful your sleep is on work nights.

(Weekends are less routine.) Please record your answer for later comparison with your results.

Answer each question Yes or No and then total your score, giving 0 points for each question on which you answered with a Yes and 2 points for each (recommended behaviour) No answer. Remember this is for work nights. Not weekends or holidays.

1. Do you go to sleep each night at different times? More than 1 hour plus or minus variance from the norm.
2, Do you drink caffeine beverages after 3 p.m.?
3. Do you drink caffeine beverages after 6 p.m.?
4. Do you have a hot bath or shower within 30 minutes of bed?
5. Do you have bright lights on in your bathroom 30 minutes or less before bedtime?
6. Does your routine vary before you go to sleep?
7. Do you watch TV within 30 minutes of bedtime?
8. Do you look at a tablet within 30 minutes of bedtime?
9. Do you look at a PC within 30 minutes of bedtime?
10. Do you look at a cell phone within 30 minutes of bedtime?
11. Do you keep a cell phone on in your bedroom at night?
12. Do you keep a tablet on in your bedroom during the night?
13. Do you eat a snack within 30 minutes of bedtime?
14. Do you keep lights on in your bedroom during the night?
15. Do you fall asleep with the television on?
16. Do you think about problems and worries at bedtime?
17. Do you snore?
18. Do you consume alcohol within 30 minutes of bedtime?
19. Do you increase the temperature of your bedroom?
20. Do you sweat at night?
21. Do you get up to urinate during the night?
22. Do you leave the radio or music on during the evening?
23. Do you have an uncomfortable pillow?
24. Do you have headaches in the morning?
25. Do you take over-the-counter sleeping medication?
26. Do you worry about the amount of sleep you are getting?

27. Do you sleep with an animal?
28. Do you sleep with a child?
29. Do you sleep with a restless partner?
30. Does your back ache?
31. Do you wake frequently during the night?
32. Do you NEVER take naps?
33. Do you think your bedroom has an unpleasant scent?
34. Do you ever fall asleep in a meeting?
35. Do you ever fall asleep at a traffic light?
36. Do you ever fall asleep when you don't want to?
37. Do you NOT drink water before bedtime?
38. Do you go to bed angry?
39. Do you take antidepressants?
40. Do you take painkillers?
41. Do you have NO exercise during the work week?
42. Do you have leg movements which wake you during the night?
43. Do you hear noises which disturb your sleep?
44. Do you eat a large evening meal?
45. Do you NEVER change your pillow?
46. Do you NEVER stretch before sleeping?
47. Do you NEVER meditate before sleeping?
48. Do you NEVER use aromatherapy such as lavender in your bedroom?
49. Do you NEVER drink herbal tea before bed?
50. Do you NEVER count your blessings and express gratitude for your life before sleeping?

If you assign 2 points for every desired NO answer you may be surprised that a score below 55 points is not UNCOMMON. If you, like most developed countries' citizens in the latest Bedroom Poll, felt that 50% of the time they had inadequate sleep or insufficient rest on work nights, you may wish to consider which of these fifty questions you can convert from YES to NO.

SWEET DREAMS!!!

10
THE EYE OF THE STORM

"You can dance in a hurricane, but only if you're standing in the eye."

Brandi Carlile

As my editors and publishers helped me review this book in the Spring/Summer of 2020, the question asked was, "how should we position Spiritual Currency Life's Capital?" They suggested that it might be appropriate in the "Self-Help" category or more probably in the "Business" section. In our training and consultations we have often explored the relationship of, "the life of business and the business of life." Considering that the world was undergoing a global pandemic with accompanying lock-downs and the inevitable negative economic consequences, the paradigm shift we are all experiencing inextricably links the help required in both life and business. While this book was not written to be only a self-help or a how to guide, it continues to be my fervent intention that we find in these contemplations, suggestions which improve our spirituality and well-being in one of the most difficult challenges of our lifetime.

The title of this chapter evokes images of hurricanes and cyclones with the inevitable Eye of the Storm, where one has survived the first wave of destructive winds and then experiences a period of calm. For most of us in the early summer of 2020 our current experience, having escaped the first wall of the viral storm, is an apt analogy for this period of transition with further dangers inevitably blowing our way.

While all of us are affected, it is my sincere hope that you and your family are able to weather the worst aspects of the Covid-19 pandemic and that these contemplations and exercises have increased our life's capital and provide a protective depository of energy.

In reviewing the book in the context of the transition from "lock down" to "return to work", this atmosphere of eerie calm and celestial clarity, where birdsong is more audible and the stars are more vibrant, is the pause which provides time to think...perhaps to "dance". *Spiritual Currency Life's Capital* is designed to provide a treasury of techniques and this crisis provides the ultimate stress test for these contemplations and their call for a conscious connectivity to our universe. With constant and confusing media messages of death and depression, like a hurricane, our "social isolation" can foment a storm of *fear* and a disconnection from all that is important to our well-being and spirituality. If the fear of the future is raising your level of ***anxiety*** then this equation may help you understand the normal emotional response which is always more pronounced during a crisis. Your ***energetic frequency*** and indeed, your spiritual currency depends on your ability to judge the ***perceived importance*** of the situation today and envision and prepare for a better tomorrow.

PERCEIVED IMPORTANCE + UNCERTAINTY = ANXIETY or the level of ENERGETIC FREQUENCY

> *"If you want to find the secrets of the universe think of energy, frequency and vibration"*
>
> *Nicola Tesla*

The compounding negative energy during this crisis is spreading like a virus of fear added to the dread of an unknown future, which is raising our collective levels of anxiety. Unfortunately, our biochemical reaction to this anxiety contributes to the physical deterioration of our immune systems, increasing our susceptibility to viral infections. So how do we control our emotions, increase our immunological health and prepare for this unknown future? Increased understanding of our emotional response comes from Professor Robert C. Bolles from the University of Washington, who studied species-specific defence reactions and avoidance learning among animals. Bolle's experiments demonstrated that the theories used to measure this emotional response were highly inaccurate. Professor Bolles argued that the species-specific defense reactions (SSDRs) were found in three basic forms: *flight, fight* (including pseudo-aggression), or *freeze*.

The quantity and spread of infections during the initial months of the Covid -19 pandemic has been shown to be directly proportional to the natural human reaction of denial, experienced throughout the world. It is this initial denial of the virus coupled with the incorrect analysis of the contagion's transmissibility which triggered the *"freeze"* emotional response, where countries delayed implementation of protocols designed to mitigate the health risk. As pandemic infections spread internationally, most governments have implemented travel prohibitions, closing borders and airports, literally, *flight* is not an option.

Almost every sound bite slogan admonishes us to *fight* the virus by staying home, which leads to terms like "lock-down" and "social-isolation." The removal of our normal freedoms increases our level of anxiety as the uncertainty of what the future will be and when we will return to normal, become less clear. As unemployment and bankruptcies grow, the instinct to *fight* with protests and pseudo aggression against the governmental prohibitions increases. Most governments are communicating chaotic and conflictive messages of how to return to work and maintain safety. Health ministers focused on prevention of Covid-19 infections are in direct conflict with the labour ministers who want to recover economic activity.

The opposing views further contribute to our collective confusion and anxiety.

Understanding our emotional response to the threats of this pandemic and indeed, any crisis, are the first steps to lower one's anxiety and preserve your life's capital, both spiritual and economic. As we weather this storm, the required separation, isolation and disconnection sap our ability to *confront* our future. *Confront* which the Oxford Dictionary defines as *to face,* is derived from the Mid 16th century French, *confronter* and further evolved from the medieval Latin, *confrontare*, (con, 'with', + frons, front, 'face'). It is our ability to *confront* which gives us resilience both immunologically and spiritually. The question is, how does one face up to the pandemic, when one is constantly bombarded with messages urging separation and avoidance of everything and everyone. It is our understanding and awareness of the dimensions of the threat of infections and positive new behaviours which will increase our ability to thrive in the future.

Our body and our spirit have the ability to become immune and resilient through understanding and positive, proactive behaviours. *"Where your attention goes your money goes,"* is a maxim which our training methodology emphasises to stress the importance of focus and connectivity. If our attention during this pandemic has focused on negative news and destructive lifestyle habits then we are diminishing our spiritual currency and our life's capital. We have explored our habits and the science of changing our behaviours throughout this book. Whether you are reading this during the *Eye of the Storm* of the Covid -19 pandemic or well after this transition phase in Spring/Summer of 2020, a brief inspection of your "lock-down" experience will help you identify the debits and credits of our ability to *confront* and react to a crisis. Please write down three positive behaviours which you have incorporated into your new routine during the weeks of "staying at home".

Did you learn something new and take some educational or training course? Possibly you focused on better physical health by increasing and improving your exercise and diet? Did you *confront* the inability to have face to face meetings with family, friends or business associates by communicating through some virtual conference application? Did you improve your environment through some D.I.Y. project or spring clean? Most importantly, did you work on the "self to self" mentioned in our chapter on communication. Write down the three favourite behaviours or accomplishments during your "stay at home" period of which you are most proud.

Recognising that some positive outcomes came from the opportunity to explore new positive behaviours helps us confront the negative repercussions of this and indeed, any crisis.

As with any inspection, our ability to recognise and indeed, *confront* our debits as well as our credits is important in understanding our reaction to the forced social isolation. Realising the small wins of positive behaviours and acts of kindness will reduce our anxiety and improve our frequency.

At the end of the first chapter you may remember the story told by George Bernard Shaw who compared the explanation of good and bad behaviours to the native American elder who had two dogs inside him. If you have "fed" your "bad" dog during the pandemic lock-down, the next exercise may help you "muzzle that dog".

Please turn to CONTEMPLATION 10: Book of Y.O.U. MUZZLE THAT DOG

The training necessary to emerge from a crisis can be encapsulated in the term coined at Whitespace, "outcreate," by which we mean to envision a positive outcome through innovative activities. To be connected, present and aware and yet to be separated and able to view a holistic future appears to be counter-intuitive. The spiritual ability to have faith in a positive future is not a fatalistic, "what will be-will be" but a historically informed perspective, aided by the evidence of humanity's inventive creativity. It is illustrative to consider the "Oracle of Omaha", Warren Buffett, when considering how to "outcreate".

Shortly after the Covid-19 pandemic precipitated 25 to 30% sell offs in most major equity markets, one of the oldest (89) and most acclaimed stock market investors, Warren Buffett, was asked to comment on the economic devastation in April of 2020. Buffet repeated one of his most famous quotes, "when the tide goes out you can see who was swimming naked." Every time since I was eleven, said Buffett, "when the financial markets have retreated, companies which were under-capitalised and poorly managed underperformed the better businesses." Buffett said his father and mother lived through the Spanish flu epidemic of 1918 and the US financial depression of 1929 and would tell him of the horrors and sadness which these crises delivered to the world. Despite the economic debilitation of the "great depression" his parents' optimism gave them enough faith in their future to conceive Warren and his older sister, Doris. Buffett incorporated his positive long term view in his investment philosophy and demonstrates surprising continued optimism considering his personal wealth fell from almost $100 billion in January of 2020 to less than $80 billion by the early summer; in direct response to the economic fallout from the pandemic.

With the perspective of hindsight, Buffett said his experience and knowledge of history provide him with the evidence of the ingenuity and intelligence of humanity. His childhood memories, combined with historical analysis, shape his understanding that many of the public health protocols in place today were positive consequences of the innovators' response to the global pandemic of 1918. Similarly, the collapse of all of the banks and peoples' life savings in the crash of 1929 precipitated the government guarantees and insurances which will protect savers today. Despite Buffett's fame as a sage of Wall Street, he argues, "the most important investment you can make is in yourself." When asked about his daily routine and to what he attributes his success, he responded, "I insist on a lot of time being spent, almost every day, to just sit and think."

I have enjoyed studying and meeting a cadre of "wise owls" and quoted their perspectives throughout this book, because experience is valuable if we wish to "outcreate". Spiritual currency in the final analysis, like all wealth is about power. The *Cambridge Dictionary* simply defines *power* as *control*. It is the *power* or other synonyms like, *capacity, ability* and *faculty* which results from the accumulation of life's capital. During the months of lock down you may have, like Warren Buffett, taken more time to think and examine what is truly essential to your spiritual, mental and physical health.

We began our journey in this book by contemplating our creation story, and taking the first steps to understand what is truly essential to our being. The ability to control and understand our personal identity builds spiritual currency and can and should be constantly re-examined.

When we have more certainty of our identities, we create a foundation for building our life's capital. I am fond of relating the importance and efficacy of self-examination in the following explanation, "certainty is clarity of observation". The introspection and examination of the evolution of our identities is an investment which compounds the return on our life's capital. If our contemplations have, as mentioned in the Second Chapter, Y.O.U, Your Own Universe, helped grow your ability and desire to become aware then you're definitely increasing your spiritual currency. It is increased mindfulness, which helps us learn as the philosopher Toffler mentions, "how to classify and reclassify information, how to evaluate its veracity". Our connectivity and understanding of our universe helps us to verify our truths, not as dogma that must be accepted but as a reality which we have created and in which we are participating. "Staying at home" became a national battle cry during the pandemic. The benefits of less air and motor traffic were soon apparent with clearer skies and less noise pollution allowing us to see stars and hear a symphony of birdsong lost in normal times. The clarity of our atmosphere allowed re-connection to stars and our environment and created a sensual re-awakening. The ability to think, while not having to commute and run between meetings should contribute to our capacity to outcreate and become a continuing habit as we return to normal life patterns.

The daily grind of our existence has been *upset* with the pandemic in 2020 and allows, indeed forces, us to change our *set-up*. As our spiritual currency grows, through reflection and observation, a reserve of energy and resolve produce a *new normal*. The speculation as to what will become our *new normal* during the summer of 2020 leads to conclusions that handshakes are unhealthy, and bowing, popular in Asian cultures may become a logical and more sanitary salutation. What we keep and what we discard in behaviours and beliefs, while more evident during a crisis-created paradigm shift, is the process of self-awareness which grows our life's capital.

Reflection, understanding and awareness cannot happen by telling students "observe, but by giving them the power and means for this observation and these means are procured through education of the senses". The Italian educator, Maria Montessori, who was also a medical doctor, understood that training one's senses was key to increasing one's understanding. So life's capital grows through increased sensual perception. The methodology we have practiced in the previous chapters can continue to develop our sensual acuity.

The major themes contained in this book's journey are *connectivity* and *awareness* and various techniques which improve our observation and understanding. It may be that our spiritual evolution is analogous to the caterpillar who frenetically consumes all of the vegetation it can, as it grows to sometimes as much as 200 times its *larval* stage. The caterpillar's function is to move, consume and grow while the resting and transition phase called *pupa* or *chrysalis* produces the metamorphosis which results in the butterfly. While one strives to evolve by accumulating our spiritual currency, the analogy of the metamorphosis to the butterfly becomes more meaningful when contemplating fractal mathematics.

It is chaos theory which embraces the unpredictability of our existence. It is the understanding of the interconnection of our social systems, ecosystems and economic systems which is theorised in fractal mathematics, which leads us back to one of chaos ∞theory's favourite metaphors, again using the butterfly. Mathematician Edward Lorenz, who pioneered chaos theory, spoke to the dynamic complexity of interrelated systems. The idea that a "butterfly could beat his wings in New Mexico and precipitate a hurricane in China," speaks to the impossibility to monitor and predict all of the systems' dynamics. Despite humanity's best efforts to produce social systems designed to analyse and protect against the ravages of public health threats, it is chaos theory which best explains our shortcomings.

While all of us hope to survive and evolve during any crisis, Eric Weiner who wrote, *The Geography of a Genius*, describes the dilemma of chaos theory. "...not all butterflies produce a hurricane, not all outbreaks of bubonic plague produce a Renaissance." In conclusion to *Spiritual Currency Life's Capital*, I would like to offer one more concept and definition which encapsulates my hope to inspire your own Renaissance, that of **exuberance**.

Exuberance is defined as *being abundantly fruitful*. The derivation of exuberance comes from the late Middle English (in the sense 'overflowing, abounding'); and further from the Latin *exuberant*-(being uber-fertile). In growing your Spiritual Currency and building your Life's Capital, it is in the final analysis, exuberance, which your investment in personal development should yield. Exuberance is often confused with enthusiasm or activity without purpose, but to the contrary, the quest to grow our spiritual currency yields the fertility which will bear fruit producing our most abundant happiness. Thank you for taking this journey and I wish you continued well-being and exuberance.

BOOK OF Y.O.U.
(YOUR OWN UNIVERSE)

INTRODUCTION

This is the book of Y.O.U. (Your Own Universe), which is designed to track and compound your life's capital. The contemplations are short, thought-provoking and easy to complete. Feel free to rewrite and edit these sessions as your self-awareness grows. Unlike other academic contemplations, there are no grades or wrong answers; so be candid and enjoy the revelations or what we like to call "aha" moments. These moments of clarity and discovery will necessarily happen more frequently as your Spiritual Currency grows and Your Own Universe reveals itself.

Contemplation 1. CREATION MYTH

Your personal "Creation Myth" is designed to relate the most important characteristics, roles and beliefs to a new acquaintance. Picture yourself having just attended an interesting function on the top floor of a skyscraper building. You and a friendly, open and non-judgemental person are waiting to board the elevator for the ride down, when he says to you, "Hello, I am Tom Wilson , I don't believe we have met," and gives you a brief description of himself which you find intriguing, the kind of person you would like to know better.

In the privacy of the elevator compartment, you now have 30 to 45 seconds to relate your "creation story" and tell Tom who you are and what is most compelling about your person.

You don't feel the need to impress him or exaggerate, and his openness and warmth puts you at ease as the lift doors close and you say: "Nice to meet you Tom, I am…"

Now please write your story. After you have finished, say it out loud and see if it takes you less than a minute. Be concise. You can edit and change as much as you want. Please feel free to return and refine your pitch. When you finish, ask yourself what roles or positions you mentioned? Have you included any which described yourself as a member of any collective group such as parent, Christian, Conservative, vegan, athlete, etc.?

This exercise should help you become aware of what you currently think is your true essence, which will necessarily evolve as you become more aware-please return often and refine your "Creation Myth". – "Pleased to meet you…"

Contemplation 2. INNER VOICE

You may never play the lottery or engage in daydreams of "if I only had", but imagine that someone gave you a winning lottery ticket or, if you prefer, a long-lost distant relative left you a life-changing inheritance. Please skip the thoughts of houses and vacations and, for that matter, any material desires and acquisitions and limit your daydreams to a list of what you would do to…

First: Change You… it can be mentally, physically, spiritually or in terms of skill development.

Second: Change the World around you…your community, your family, your friends, etc. While the money may empower you, try and focus on your active participation not passive charitable donations.

Now please choose one that with work, organisation and intention you might begin to change, even without the windfall. Please note your selection for later reference.

Contemplation 3. MINDFULNESS

> *"...there is nothing either good or bad but thinking makes it so."*
>
> *Hamlet*

It is an ironic contradiction in terms that by emptying one's mind through meditation techniques one can achieve "mindfulness". It is, however, now proven through the latest neuroscientific studies that actual physical changes in the human brain can be produced by practising meditation. You may have tried a variety of techniques to meditate and even gone so far to acquire a "mantra" or short phrase which can be silently chanted while trying to achieve the desired stillness in one's mind? One of my clients, who believed in the efficacy of meditation and had the intention to improve his focus, would fall asleep after repeating his mantra for a few minutes. Sleep is not the goal, although many people meditate before sleeping to relax themselves. Others start their day with a meditation. Find the time appropriate to your lifestyle and responsibilities.

Many other people find it difficult to be still. If you have the positive habit of meditating and are comfortable with your techniques, congratulations; keep increasing your awareness and adding to your spiritual currency. Longer meditation periods are desirable, time permitting, so keep going.

The simplest and shortest meditation technique is to find a quiet place, inevitably there will always be some sounds, and your awareness of them is a positive expansion of your consciousness and desirable. Now sit comfortably; no lotus position is required unless you have incredible flexibility; a normal chair or sofa is perfectly fine. Attempt to achieve stillness and empty your mind of thoughts for a short time, initially of up to 4 to 5 minutes. Check your clock before and after you meditate and attempt longer periods each day. Like all habits try to make this a daily practice and if you miss a day, don't worry, return to your intention and continue. When after a few weeks your body and mind crave this stillness, it has become a habit and will increase your focus, reduce your stress and add to your life's capital.

TECHNIQUE: Now sitting comfortably, close your eyes and take a deep cleansing breath in through your nostrils and feel the temperature of the air, the smell of the room, the sound of the breath as you inhale. After filling your lungs, purse your lips and exhale slowly, again listening to the sound of the escaping air, experiencing all your involved senses of touch, smell and hearing. Now breathe normally, not too deep or too shallow, but naturally in through your nose and out through your pursed lips. Listen to the sound of your breathing, and concentrate on the sounds. If you concentrate and listen, it will help empty your mind from distractions and thoughts of our daily worries and obligations. When a thought pops into your mind, chase it away by listening more intently to the sound of your breathing. The object is **not** to think, but to empty your mind and achieve mental stillness.

As one is listening to one's breathing, inevitably a sound will arouse our curiosity. If you can't quickly identify it, such as the heating or air-conditioning machines, unless it is an alarming sound, such as a baby's cry, a dog's bark, etc., push it away by promising to think about it later.

I hope you find this meditation, simple and refreshing. Feel free to experiment with the variety of techniques and applications available to find your best combination. YouTube and Spotify have many soothing "white" noises which may help.

Contemplation 4. SENSES

The human consciousness has evolved to help in our survival. The way we employ our senses has necessarily developed to help our brain perceive the world around us. It is commonly accepted that humans have five senses: sight, hearing, smell, touch and taste. Modern science continues to debate the human sensory capacity and compares and contrasts our abilities to the rest of the animal kingdom. Expressions like the "eye of an eagle", or the "nose of a bloodhound", quite correctly recognise the inferiority of human sight and smell when compared to those animals.

The latest neuroscientific research includes two important senses which have been the biggest challenge to duplicate in Artificial Intelligence-driven robots. These senses are called "vestibular" and "proprioception".' Our bodies' vestibular system allows one to feel gravity, movement and balance. Our inner ear is the organ which helps in this gyroscopic ability to know when we are lying down or sitting up or when we are moving in an elevator or car. It is this perception of yourself in relation to our surroundings which is most difficult for Artificial Intelligence to comprehend. Bats use the vestibular sense of echolocation to such a degree that while flying they can detect an insect at over 30 feet away and capture it without using normal vision.

Proprioception is the sense of our individual body parts, and their relative position and employed strength of effort for each movement, which is often called coordination. One's ability to walk in a straight line or touch the index fingers of both hands with one's eyes closed are two examples of human proprioception. The loss of proprioception is often evidenced with states of inebriation and police enforcement methods typically employ movement tests, like walking with one foot in front of the other, as an indicator of the suspect's level of intoxication. Alcohol limits the human sense of proprioception and those limits are directly proportional to the level of inebriation.

This next exercise is designed to heighten one's awareness of your surroundings and to sharpen your senses. This exercise is adapted from my friend Mary's family game and can be conducted with one or more participants. I commented to Mary one day that she had an amazing ability to stay in the moment and absorb and understand her environment. Mary stated that her presence and sensory abilities were developed in part by competing with her five siblings in pursuit of pudding or dessert. With my curiosity duly piqued, I asked Mary to explain.

Mary, the second of six children, who were all less than two years apart in age, stated that 1960s Britain was an environment where "youngsters were meant to be seen but not heard". Mary's mother created a game which would require all six of her school age children to focus, be calm and present, and necessarily silent. This game would demand of each child to engage their senses and attempt to remember the perceptions noticed in the first few minutes, when entering a restaurant. Mary's mother would define the game as a memory contest but in reality, it required each child to sharpen their sensory perceptions.

The game would start as the family was waiting to be seated, and the children were instructed to look carefully at the restaurant surroundings and use all of their senses to absorb every possible detail. Mary said that, after the family were seated, her mother would say, "Now close your eyes tightly and any peeking will mean immediate forfeit of any pudding." The questions would start with the easiest to the youngest and became increasingly more difficult as the older children were queried. The littlest sister would be asked what colour is the carpet? The questions would ask about colours or design or smells or feels, all the while with the children's eyes tightly closed. Mary laughed and said that it was almost always one of the older children who would be asked a question that they would be unable to answer and thus be penalised with the loss of dessert. Soon thereafter the waitress would appear with menus and the children would congratulate the winners and commiserate with the losers.

From child to child the questions would progress, such as "What colour is the waitress's dress?"… "What shape is the mirror on the far wall?"... "What smell do you recognise?"... "What sound can you hear outside?"... "What did the menu feel like?" etc. By forcing the children to close their eyes, their other senses, those of smell, hearing, touch and taste, are necessarily heightened. Details to be seen in the brief initial viewing of the restaurant space are always more recognised with the incentives of the competition, and people with more awareness have a greater sense and enjoyment of their environment.

In order to challenge your senses, the next time you are waiting for a table with a friend, ask them to play the game. Tell them you are going to look at every detail and use all of your senses to experience your environment. Ask them to quiz you while you close your eyes and see to what level of detail you can remember the surroundings. Make a mental note of smells and sensations you would not normally experience without the extra attention produced by your increased awareness.

Please note your experience and record which senses were engaged and which senses demonstrated more or less acuity.

Contemplation 5. MASKS & Y.O.U. (Your Own Universe)

In every culture and, on every continent, humans have used masks to protect and, in some cases, heal their spirits. Modern humans in a less ritualistic manner continue to use masks to remain anonymous, or at least to appear different from their real persona. In Contemplation 1 you may remember your brief introduction to describe yourself. Please take time now to return to this first exercise and examine every descriptive term you used to explain yourself by circling those adjectives and qualifications. Were any of the terms circled part of a collective group? As an example, did you mention you were a parent or sibling? Did you mention your heritage or race or ethnicity? Did you mention your position in a company – Director or Chairman, etc.? One may be perfectly honest and justifiably proud of one's work or educational attainments, but still hiding behind masks which allow us to protect our *true* identity.

Now ask yourself if any of the descriptive terms are a shield or mask? If so, what are you hiding and why? Remember, this is your confidential workbook; so take time to introspect and enhance your self-awareness by being critically analytical and brutally honest. Please record your findings.

Personal honesty and identification of our various masks then begs the question of how to improve our persona in order to require fewer layers of protection and achieve comfort with our real essence.

Oprah Winfrey was heard to relate a story regarding her ample experience in meeting and interviewing some of the world's most important people, which is relevant to our pursuit of identifying our personal masks. Oprah said that after interviewing over 10,000 significant people, it never ceases to amaze her that without fail they will ask her something like "How was that... or How did I do?" No matter how confident or charismatic even the most seasoned media stars are aware that they may have removed some of their masks and demonstrate concern for their self-image and, indeed, for their performance.

Contemplation 6. BELIEF SYSTEM

We all have a belief system from which we operate. If we can agree that our current understanding of what we believe as our foundational principles has evolved and will continue to improve with inspection, then this exercise will challenge you to articulate your beliefs and continue that evolution. One can accrue additional Spiritual Currency and add to our Life's Capital by discarding beliefs which lead to undesirable outcomes and accepting beliefs which assist us in confronting life's travails and disappointments. Humans have developed guiding principles based on our environment which includes our parents and family, our society, including our education, our culture, which includes our civic membership, which may define and codify proper behaviour. These community ideals, as well as our religion and or philosophy, which may have imbued us with core beliefs, are a composite of our life's experience. VIRTUE is defined as *moral excellence* and something *to be valued*. What do you believe to be valuable?

This exercise is simple in construct but may necessarily require frequent updating, as our priorities change with additional insights and environmental influences evolve our perception of moral excellence.

Please find a list below of ten virtues which is by no means exhaustive or necessarily the most important virtues. This list has been compiled by selecting traits or qualities which are valued as fundamental principles to attain a morally good life.

Please rank in importance from 1 to 10 the virtues you consider to be most important. Feel free to substitute other terms or qualities which may be more important to you than this list which contains very Western philosophical and religious ideals. As an example, courage or bravery is valued by both Western and Eastern philosophies, while mindfulness, which includes mental ability and awareness, is more important to Eastern philosophies. The more we are exposed to different prescriptions to attain excellence and moral goodness, the more we can adapt and improve our personal belief system. Please select any more important virtues to compile your top ten.

Ten virtues to rank after substituting any personal preferences to the following. There is no "right" answer, but the reflection will enhance your morality and improve your self-awareness.

__ Courage
__ Hope
__ Love
__ Justice
__ Prudence/self-control
__ Truth/honesty
__ Mindfulness
__ Kindness/charity
__ Equanimity/balance
__ Diligence

Other popular choices may include, humility, patience, reflection, forgiveness, responsibility, non-violence, thriftiness, joyfulness, compassion, productivity, loyalty.

Contemplation 7. PARADIGM EXAMINATION

"What are our top three, **DREAMS** or **INTENTIONS**?" You may wonder, "why only three?" and my answer would be, whatever you think is your most important goal, may change by the mere examination of the **INTENTION**.

Think Big – no, **BIGGER**! Now go for it... write down your three intentions and follow the steps of the four columns.

ENVISION is the creation, actually or in our mind, of a mock-up of what our ambition looks like... model it, draw it if you can.

STRATEGY is the second column which is logically created to build or achieve our visualisation. What's the strategy or plan? How? By when?

IMPLEMENT is the execution of our "plan" as modelled.

OUTCOME or result is the fourth and last column which is produced by our accurately modelled and well-planned implementation of our intention. Visualise your success... feel it.

Contemplation 8. IDENTIFY YOUR PASSION

Upon the death of their citizens, the ancient Greeks asked the question: "Did he live a life of passion?" While death is not a pleasant contemplation, the following exercise is designed to have you identify and articulate your most important life's purpose.

You may have wandered through a cemetery or church graveyard. The tombstones are illustrative of lives that are sometimes all too brief and others that are incredibly lengthy. Often one finds epitaphs on gravestones which state mother, daughter, etc., denoting the relationship to the surviving mourners. Other epitaphs are recorded at the behest of the deceased and, by means of an interesting anecdote, sometimes record the humour and wit of the interred.

The American comedian Rodney Dangerfield has etched on his tombstone: "There goes the neighbourhood." Dangerfield's passion for humour is evidenced for all to see, even after his passing. The iconic British Prime Minister Winston Churchill, known for his wit, requested the following in his epitaph: "I am ready to meet my maker. Whether my maker is prepared for the great ordeal of meeting me is another matter." Another humorous epitaph, yet indicative of the passion of the deceased, is seen on the grave marker of the Rock and Roll Hall of Fame musician, Dee Dee Ramone. The most famous hit of his punk rock band, The Ramones,

'Blitzkrieg Bop', contains the iconic lyrics "Go now". His marker says, "OK… I gotta go now."

Please take a few minutes to write your epitaph, and while you may list various achievements, degrees, awards and offspring and be justifiably proud of all, the main objective is to identify and articulate that about which you are most passionate.

Contemplation 9. DOG FOOD

We all have positive and negative inclinations which the Native Americans described as "two dogs" within us, which we "feed". This exercise is designed to identify this duality in three areas: 1st **HEALTH**, 2nd **RELATIONSHIPS**, 3rd **MONEY**. You may wish to choose other important aspects of your life and identify this duality but at least examine these initial three areas. The exercise is designed to select the best and worst **daily** habits or behaviours which shape our existence. Which "dog" are you feeding?

As an example you may choose in **HEALTH:**

BEST: Exercising daily   WORST: Smoking daily

OR

BEST: Eating nutritious meals WORST: Eating too much sugar and desserts

OR

BEST: Daily meditation   WORST: Keeping the phone next to me while I sleep

As mentioned previously, there is no correct or even preferable answer, but identify a **daily** behaviour which you believe is positive and one that is related to the positive habit but unfortunately negative. Analogous to the way one looks at saving and spending habits and attempts to increase income and wealth accumulation while managing and lowering expenses, desirable and undesirable behaviours are often ignored. Unfortunately, the human mind allows positive habits to go unrecognised and negative habits to become addictive, in the sense of truly harmful to our well-being. Identification and realisation of our best and worst habits are the first steps to reinforcing positive behaviour and eliminating negative habits. This exercise is designed to help one "know what they don't know".

HEALTH
BEST: WORST:

RELATIONSHIPS
BEST: WORST:

MONEY
BEST: WORST:

Contemplation 10. MUZZLE AND REWARD YOUR DOG

You will have seen dogs with a muzzle, as you walk in a park. As a dog owner and lover, I know that many times these muzzles are a way to change unwanted behaviours like eating undesirable things on the ground and not necessarily because the dog is aggressive and bites. Similarly, this next exercise follows on from the previous "DOG FOOD" exercise, where you have identified the "WORST" habits or negative behaviours and is designed to reduce or "muzzle" that behaviour to prevent the feeding and reinforcement of unwanted activities.

You may have a preconceived notion that a negative habit is impossible to change, given your genetic and psychological predisposition. You may also have read or believe that it takes as little as three weeks to embed a new habit, or change or muzzle an undesirable behaviour. Social scientists have argued the required habit forming length of time, since the plastic surgeon, Maxwell Maltz wrote his popular book *Psycho-Cybernetics* in 1960. Having observed that it took on average 3 weeks for amputees to lose the "ghost limb" feeling, Maltz posited that 21 days was the required average time to form a habit.

My work and observation with clients who suffer some stress is that habits can form almost immediately and become more pernicious and difficult to muzzle dependent on factors including severity, repetition, frequency and reinforcement of the behaviour. Sensitivity to loud noises is one undesirable habit which is observed in clients who suffer automobile accidents and even in dogs after hearing loud fireworks. Sound sensitivity is even faster and more difficult to arrest in PTS (Post Traumatic Stress) patients who may have suffered the effects of an explosion. In any case, the good news is whatever behaviour you wish to change, the longer you can perform the new action, even if you lapse or miss the occasional day, the greater chance that your behaviour will become a habit.

The latest study performed by the University College of London and published in the European Journal of Social Psychology has proven that a new habit is formed on average in 66 days. Rather than worry about how many days, take the first step. It is your intention and commitment, which will muzzle unwanted behaviours, despite the occasional failures or lapses, if one starts again over time your habits can change.

While we all can appreciate positive reinforcement, which when training dogs is given in the form of a food reward, all too often humans tend to ignore their own progress when attempting to eradicate an undesirable habit and even when a positive activity is practiced. For the purposes of the exercise chose **one** undesirable activity you would like to muzzle or eliminate and **one** new positive habit you would like to form.

Choose an appropriate reward and track your progress and the positive reinforcement which celebrates your wins on a weekly basis.

Negative Habit to Muzzle, Reduce or Eliminate:

_____

Positive Habit to Form and Reward:

_____

Example: Negative Habit to Muzzle SUGAR CONSUMPTION

If you have, as most members of Western society, a propensity to consume refined sugars and agree that it is important to reduce if not eliminate this habit, then you will be interested in the latest studies by American Psychiatrist Judson Brewer. The science of the effects of mindfulness on the brain are overwhelming in their proof that increased awareness can help overcome habits which are ingrained due to evolutionary survival programming.

The human survival instinct has developed as a natural reward-based learning process, based on positive and negative reinforcement. In the case of sugar one can comprehend that most fruits when ripened have a sweet taste which has triggered our brains with the programme.

See Food → **Eat Food** → **Repeat**
and with sugars **Trigger** → **Behaviour** → **Reward**

Positive and negative reinforcements, including the genetically evolved program that sweet fruits are nutritious and digestible and are to be preferred to bitter unripe fruits which may produce digestive upsets. Survival instincts have caused a natural reward-based learning process which rewards the consumption of sweet foods and the human predisposition to avoid bitter tastes.

Mindfulness allows one to move from knowledge to wisdom. It is awareness or cognitive control from the prefrontal cortex which is the last part of the brain to evolve in humans and permits us to control our behaviours. Mindfulness and meditation, but for now the knowledge that our most pernicious behaviours can be muzzled by increased awareness of the activity, will assist in your quest to eliminate unwanted habits.

The mindfulness technique of Judson Brewer calls for patients to examine their feelings and physical manifestations when participating in the unwanted activity with what he terms "curious awareness". Brewer's studies demonstrate that mindfulness increases the human mind's ability to break bad habits by increasing awareness. He states mindfulness increases our ability to be curious and that allows us "...to notice that cravings are simply made up of body sensations which we can manage when we step into being... there's tightness, there's tension, there's restlessness and that these body sensations... we can manage from moment to moment rather than to be clobbered by this huge scary craving... when we step out of our fear based habit patterns and we step into being."

So, in your quest to form positive habits and eliminate unwanted behaviours develop a "curious awareness" of your emotional and physical responses to the behaviours and celebrate the wins you have achieved by reinforcing the habit by a just reward. By just reward, I don't mean celebrate your successful reduction of sugar by consuming a pint of ice cream but by positively rewarding yourself with a small trophy of clothing or electronics that gives you tangible feedback that you are making progress.

Thanks for completing the exercises; it is my intention that your self-awareness has expanded and your connectivity to your universe has intensified...Keep becoming more Y.O.U.?

ACKNOWLEDGEMENTS

This conversation has been inspired and enriched by many friends, clients and teachers who have encouraged me to consolidate my thoughts in book form. I am most grateful for their friendship, insights and contributions. I am especially thankful for the generous patronage and inspirational discussions from Viscount Christopher Portman which led to the London Leadership Centre and which contributed to the evolution of the Whitespace community.

My clients have in many cases become friends, and I am especially grateful for Bjorn Bayley (IKEA Foundation) for the growth of the Whitespace community and publication of *Spiritual Currency: Life's Capital*. I also would like to thank J. T. Taylor for his research and suggestions and his mother Mary Joan Salkeld Taylor who performed many useful edits, may she rest in peace. And finally to my publishers and editors at University of Buckingham Press my heartfelt gratitude for their patient guidance.